The Wit & Wisdom of Oscar Wilde

The Wit & Wisdom of Oscar Wilde

A Treasury of Quotations, Anecdotes, and Observations

Ralph Keyes

Gramercy Books
New York

This 1999 edition is published by Gramercy Books, an imprint of Random House Value Publishing, a division of Random House, Inc., New York, by arrangement with Doe Coover Agency, Winchester, Mass.

Gramercy is a registered trademark and the colophon is a trademark of Random House, Inc.

Random House
New York • Toronto • London • Sydney • Auckland
www.randomhouse.com

Printed and bound in the United States of America.

Library of Congress Cataloging-in-Publication Data

Wilde, Oscar, 1854–1900.
　　The wit & wisdom of Oscar Wilde : a treasury of quotations,
anecdotes, and observations / [compiled and edited by] Ralph Keyes.
　　　　p.　　　cm.
　　Originally published: New York : HarperCollins, ©1996.
　　Includes bibliographical references and index.
　　ISBN 0-517-19460-0
　　1. Wilde, Oscar, 1854–1900 Quotations.　I. Keyes, Ralph.
II. Title.　III. Title: Wit and wisdom of Oscar Wilde.
[PR5812.K49　1999]
828'.809—dc21
　　　　　　　　　　　　　　　　　　　99-14881
　　　　　　　　　　　　　　　　　　　CIP

8　7

For Pat Gershwin,
my mother's friend,
and mine

Contents

Acknowledgments

I would like to acknowledge help from the staffs of the Yellow Springs and Antioch College libraries—Jan Miller especially—for assistance with research, and Lee Huntington and Walter Rhodes for manuscript review.

My agent, Colleen Mohyde, and editors Hugh Van Dusen and Katherine Ekrem supported me throughout this project. My wife Muriel gave me her usual invaluable help with research, manuscript criticism, and by creating the setting that made it possible to complete this project.

Author's Note

*I*n his fine book *The Quote Sleuth,* Anthony Shipps writes of Oscar Wilde, "There is a great need for a definitive, well-indexed, well-referenced collection of his witticisms and other gems." I hope this volume meets that need. The few compilations of Wilde's sayings already published were intended for English readers of another era. Such collections vary widely in reliability. Most compilers of Wilde's work felt little compunction about revising his words: adding here, subtracting there, polishing up what they thought might be dull.

No word of Wilde's has been changed in this compilation. To the contrary, by using original sources whenever possible—including material not only from Wilde's plays, essays, and fiction but also from his more obscure reviews, letters to the editor, and appearances in friends' memoirs—I've sometimes been able to restore Wilde's actual words when others took the liberty of rewriting them.

As is customary in compilations of this kind, I have made minor alterations of Oscar Wilde's form for the sake of consistency and clarity. Occasional words added to clarify a remark are put in brackets. British spelling has been converted to American. Wilde's random and inconsistent capitalization—part of his literary *esprit*—hasn't been touched. Some throat-clearing words or phrases ("I need hardly say that," "You know," etc.) have been deleted. Deletions within quotations are indicated by ellipses. For the sake of visual grace I have capitalized words at the outset of sentences whose actual beginning has been pruned, and put periods at the end of some with edited endings. This has all been done for reading ease, and to best convey Oscar Wilde's thinking.

The Wit & Wisdom of Oscar Wilde

The Puzzle of Oscar Wilde

> If, with the literate, I am
> Impelled to try an epigram,
> I never seek to take the credit;
> We all assume that Oscar said it.
>
> —DOROTHY PARKER

> He left behind, as his essential contribution to literature,
> a large repertoire of jokes which survive because of their
> sheer neatness, and because of a certain intriguing uncer-
> tainty—which extends to Wilde himself—as to whether
> they really mean anything.
>
> —GEORGE ORWELL

Nearly a century since his death, what shall we make of Oscar Wilde? Was Wilde merely a bright boy in a man's body or a thoughtful prophet cleverly wrapping profundity in dazzling verbal giftwrap? Until his trials for "gross indecency," this puzzle intrigued Victorian England. From the time he packed his blue china to leave Oxford for London in 1879 until his imprisonment sixteen years later, Wilde's contemporaries never knew how

I

seriously to take him. During his two years in prison, they stopped wondering. Oscar Wilde's books were withdrawn from circulation and his plays canceled.

It didn't take long, however, for the fickle public to renew its interest in Oscar Wilde. A decade after his death at age forty-six in 1900, Wilde's bankrupt estate was flush. By World War II more Europeans read Wilde than they did any English writer except Shakespeare. Today he is the only author of his time and place who still has a broad following. Oscar Wilde's writing remains fresh, alive, electric. His words stride off the page to grab us by the lapel and demand that we pay attention. "You've got to listen to what I'm about to tell you," they insist. And we do; gladly. Wilde's claim to our attention has kept *The Picture of Dorian Gray* continuously in print for over a century, *The Importance of Being Earnest* repeatedly staged, and *The Happy Prince* revived onto the bestseller list. "He is not one of those writers who as the centuries change lose their relevance," observed biographer Richard Ellmann. "Wilde is one of us."

It wasn't just Wilde's writing that was ahead of its time. His disdain for conventional morality and relentless pursuit of celebrity broke ground later tilled by counterparts ranging from Truman Capote to Andy Warhol. Wilde was an advance herald of existentialism, and the intellectual godfather of '60s "flower children." As aestheticism's most prominent advocate, he helped create a climate receptive to Europe's contemporary design revolution. For better or worse, his contention that criticism could be an art form encouraged subsequent critics to follow Wilde's lead and impose themselves on whatever they were ostensibly criticizing.

More than anything else, it is the sum of Oscar Wilde's forty-six years that commands our attention. Wilde felt that way himself. "Do you want to know the great drama of my life?" he asked André Gide. "It's that I have put my genius into my life; all I've put into my works is my talent." Wilde's life was an ongoing performance starring himself. Writing was merely a vehicle propelling him toward his real goal: the dramatization of Oscar Wilde.

Men of Wilde's size (a bulky six-foot-three) typically dress down to take the edge off their imposing physical presence. Oscar dressed up. He wore knee breeches, red waistcoats, velvet jackets, and a massive fur coat. A hairdresser waved his hair daily. He chain-smoked gold-tipped cigarettes. His ring featured a large green beetle. The buttonhole of his jacket was invariably decorated with some expensive flower.

Wilde was unapologetic about his flamboyant hunger for attention. "Somehow or other I'll be famous, and if not famous I'll be notorious," he told an Oxford classmate. After leaving Oxford for London, Wilde pioneered the use of mass media for self-advertisement. He routinely wrote witty letters in duplicate, one for his correspondent, one for the press. By continually satirizing this easy target, *Punch* became Oscar Wilde's faithful publicist. So did Gilbert and Sullivan when they featured a Wilde-like fop named Reginald Bunthorne in their comic opera *Patience*. Londoners laughed, but they paid attention. As would be true of Dorothy Parker in New York half a century later, retailing Oscar's latest *mot* was quite the fashion in Victorian London. "Every omnibus-conductor knew his latest jokes," said Wilde's friend Ada Leverson.

Talking was Wilde's vocation, writing his avocation. Those who knew him were virtually unanimous that Oscar Wilde was the best conversationalist they'd ever met. Shaw thought him "the greatest talker of his time—perhaps of all time." Sir Max Beerbohm—who'd heard such other masters of table talk as Henry James, Gilbert Chesterton, and Hilaire Belloc—said none could compare to Wilde. "Oscar in *his* own way was the greatest of them all—" said Beerbohm, "the most spontaneous and yet the most polished, the most soothing and yet the most surprising."

During his 1882 lecture tour of America, Wilde was invited to visit an artists' studio in San Francisco. As a lark, the artists' wives had dressed up a female portrait dummy, complete with gloves and a fan. This mannequin was dubbed "Miss Piffle." While touring the studio, Wilde bumped into her. Backing up with a bow, he apologized for the mishap. Without missing a beat, Wilde proceeded to give Miss Piffle his impressions of America. He related some funny anecdotes and replied to her imagined comments with clever repartee. "It was a superb performance, a masterpiece of sparkling wit and gaiety," marveled an onlooker. "Never before, or since, have I heard anything that compared to it."

Unlike many a great monologist, Wilde didn't deny others the opportunity to join him in conversation. Few dared. To engage Wilde in a dialogue would have been like playing tennis with Martina Navratilova or dancing with Fred Astaire. Or perhaps dueling with Cyrano de Bergerac. While courtly and considerate, Wilde could also be cutting. He was a master of the veiled barb. The deftness and subtlety of Wilde's malice made it no less malicious; the sharpness of his stiletto didn't dull the pain of its wound. Wilde's observation that Shaw had no enemies, but none of his friends liked him, was clever, mean, and wrong. So was his contention that an upwardly mobile acquaintance "came to London in hopes of founding a salon and succeeded in opening a saloon." (Wilde repeated this quip in *The Picture of Dorian Gray*.) The same thing could be said of Oscar Wilde that he wrote about a character in *Vera:* "He would stab his best friend for the sake of writing an epigram on his tombstone."

Like Twain, Churchill, and so many others renowned for spontaneous wit, Wilde kept carefully crafted quips in his pocket, waiting for the proper moment to launch them into conversation. He couldn't always wait, however, and was notorious for setting conversational traps in which to spring a new epigram. Wilde once asked a friend named Coulson Kernahan about his religious convictions. Kernahan responded in all seriousness. When he had finished, Wilde said with a smile, "You are so evidently, so unmistakably sincere and most of all so truthful, that . . . I can't believe a single word you say."

Kernahan later recalled Wilde's countenance in the aftermath of this volley:

Having discharged his missile, Wilde, no longer lolling indolently forward in his seat, pulled himself backwards, and up like a gunner taking a pace to the rear, or the side of his gun the better to see the crash of the shell upon the target, and then, if I may so word it, "smiled all over." He was so openly, so provokingly pleased with himself and with this particular paradox that not to be a party to the gratification of such sinful vanity, instead of complimenting him, as he had expected, on its neatness, I ignored the palpable hit, and inquired:

> *"Where are you dining tonight, Wilde?"*
>
> *"At the Duchess of So-and-So's," he answered.*
>
> *"Precisely. Who is the guest you have marked down, upon whom—when everybody is listening—to work off that carefully prepared impromptu wheeze about 'You are so truthful that I can't believe a single word you say,' which you have just fired off on me?"*
>
> *Wilde sighed deeply and threw out his hands with a gesture of despair, but the ghost of a glint of a smile in the corner of his eye signaled a bull's eye to me.*

Those who had heard Wilde talk found reading his written words disappointing—rather like drinking yesterday's wine. The words were there, but the spirit was missing: the lilt, the sparkle, the daring leaps from one topic to the next. Some of Wilde's best lines occurred only during conversation. "One must have a heart of stone to read the death of Little Nell without laughing," for example—like so many of Wilde's quips—appears nowhere in his published work. (This one was jotted down by Ada Leverson.)

By mixing the insights in some of his essays with the witty dialogue in *The Importance of Being Earnest*, suggested his friend Adela Schuster, one could get a hint of his conversational prowess. This prowess was built on a foundation of epigrams. "One never left him without carrying away some characteristic *mot*," said the poet Richard Le Gallienne, "light as thistledown, yet usually pregnant with meaning." Oscar Wilde was the leading aphorist of his era, and among the best of all time. He was well equipped not only with the conviction but with the glibness and audacity that aphorizing calls for. The spirit of brash certainty that is aphorizing's lifeblood can be hard to sustain. Wilde was up to the challenge. Until his final years, he seldom hesitated to be categorical. "I still recall perfect sayings of his," said the painter Will Rothenstein, "as perfect now as on the day when he said them."

By his own choice, Wilde's commentary was more often witty than wise. Many of his epigrams were little more than wordplay. They suggest a precocious teenager showing off for bemused grownups.

  ℝ Familiarity breeds consent.

  ℝ Nothing succeeds like excess.

  ℝ It is better to be good-looking than to be good.

  ℝ I can believe anything, provided that it is quite incredible.

Did Wilde know what he was about? Of course he did. "I throw probability out of the window for the sake of a phrase," Wilde told Arthur Conan Doyle, "and the chance of an epigram makes me desert truth."

Because he was so smart, even Wilde's flip remarks implied insight, as if by chewing on their husk long enough one might reach a kernel of wisdom. For all of their verbal hijinks, many of Wilde's observations displayed real perception. Amid the glitter of his wit lay nuggets of insight.

  ℝ The reason we all like to think so well of others is that we are all afraid for ourselves. The basis of optimism is sheer terror.

  ℝ We think that we are generous because we credit our neighbor with the possession of those virtues that are likely to be a benefit to us.

✍ No man dies for what he knows to be true. Men die for what they want to be true, for what some terror in their hearts tells them is not true.

✍ Anybody can sympathize with the sufferings of a friend, but it requires a very fine nature . . . to sympathize with a friend's success.

One reason Oscar Wilde so baffled his contemporaries—as he does us—was that he freely mingled such wisdom with mere frippery. Reading his work is like touring an art gallery in which works by Red Grooms, Pablo Picasso, and Charles Schulz are hung side by side. Like so many brilliant men, Wilde took for granted that his listeners and readers were as able as he was to juggle many perspectives at once. When waxing paradoxical for sheer recreation, he assumed others were in on the joke. Wilde knew that he often just played with words, toyed with ideas, struck poses. He was as charmed as anyone by the performance. "Wilde has been the life and soul of the voyage," said a fellow passenger on his 1882 crossing to New York. "He has showered good stories and *bon mots*, paradoxes and epigrams upon me all the way, while he certainly has a never-failing bonhomie which makes him roar with laughter at his own absurd theories and conceits."

Oscar enjoyed amusing and amazing so much that it wasn't always clear when he was being serious. Nor did he care to say. "To the world I seem, by intention on my part, a dilettante and dandy merely—" he once wrote a friend, "it is not wise to show one's heart to the world—and as seriousness of manner is the disguise of the fool, folly . . . is the robe of the wise man." As part of his outrageous persona, Wilde considered honesty an overrated virtue. He regarded any attempt to pin him down about the veracity of his views as a sure sign of a limited intellect. During his first trial, when quizzed about a saying he'd written, Wilde said airily, "I think it is an amusing paradox, an amusing play on words." Challenged about the truth of another epigram, he responded, "I rarely think that anything I write is true."

The writer Sir Henry Newbolt once watched Wilde discuss the virtues of some obscure Elizabethan playwrights, with frequent citation of their work. Newbolt was so impressed by Wilde's peroration that he jotted down some of his references in order to look them up later. He could find none of the plays cited. Nor could Newbolt locate any of the "playwrights" Wilde had so learnedly discussed. They existed only in his fertile imagination. "My feeling was chiefly one of almost awed surprise at his wonderful powers—" said Newbolt, "the imitations were so perfect and so striking in themselves as to be worthy of the forged names he appended to them."

Wilde loved to create verbal works of art. To him, inquiring about their truthfulness was like quizzing a painter about the validity of his reds or blues. Wilde routinely said things he didn't mean because they sounded pretty. Did he really believe that "Men who are dandies and women who are darlings rule the world, at least they should do so"? I doubt it. More likely he was delighted by the resonance of "dandy" and "darling" in such close juxtaposition. Elsewhere, Wilde juxtaposed "kisses and blisses," "scribblers and nibblers," and commended a book for substituting "the vice of verbosity for the stupidity of silence."

Friends noted how often Wilde repeated the same phrases, albeit honed, sharpened, polished. Like a stand-up comedian, he continually recycled good lines. Wilde's sayings moved freely from conversation to essay to fiction to drama. Sometimes they moved freely from other people's conversation. His quip "If one had the money to go to America, one would not go," was based on a friend's earlier question, "Who would go to Australia if he had the money to go with?" Another famous Wildeism—"Good Americans, when they die, go to Paris"—appeared first in Oliver Wendell Holmes's *Autocrat of the Breakfast-Table.* So did "Give me the luxuries, and anyone can have the necessaries," a line later attributed to Wilde.

Wilde borrowed other people's material without apologies. "I appropriate what is already mine," he explained, "for once a thing is published it becomes public property." His sometime friend James Whistler rarely missed an opportunity to accuse Wilde of blatant theft on the high literary seas. After Whistler got off a good line, the painter said Wilde told him, "I wish I'd said that."

"You will, Oscar, you will," Whistler retorted.

Wilde, Whistler concluded, "has the courage of the opinions of others." Wilde responded by using this aphorism without attribution in a subsequent essay.

But aphorisms are a revolving fund. Even as Wilde withdrew, he deposited far more than his share of lasting epigrams. In his play *An Ideal Husband,* Wilde included the thought that "Life is never fair," perhaps inspiring John F. Kennedy's similar observation seventy years later. Wilde's "I can resist everything except temptation" was later attributed to Mark Twain, Mae West, and W. C. Fields. In *Man and Superman,* Shaw wrote, "There are two tragedies in life. One is to lose your heart's desire. The other is to gain it." A decade earlier, in *Lady Windermere's Fan,* Wilde observed, "In this world there are only two tragedies. One is not getting what one wants, and the other is getting it."

A key problem facing any compiler of Oscar Wilde's sayings is selecting the best from an embarrassment of riches. Harvesting aphorisms from Wilde's canon is like fly-fishing in a fish farm. Wilde put so many maxims into his writing that we have a wealth of them on the record. His play scripts were basically a bulletin board on which Wilde pinned his best remarks. The comedies in particular featured one quip after another mouthed by characters— men and women alike—who were thinly disguised depictions of the playwright's various facets. Scene-setting, character development, and plot were essentially filler. The playwright conceded that his characters did very little. Like their creator, he said, they were content to "sit in chairs and chatter."

It may be true that authors shouldn't be held accountable for the views of their characters. But the narcissistic Wilde was not one to create fictional figures distinct from himself. Because Wilde's writing was largely a forum for his own observations, one is usually safe in taking his characters' views as Wilde's. If such views were often inconsistent and contradictory, so was their author.

✍ Details are always vulgar.

✍ Details are the only things that interest.

——

✍ To be modern is the only thing worth being nowadays.

✍ Nothing is so dangerous as being too modern; one is apt to grow old-fashioned quite suddenly.

——

✍ The supreme vice is shallowness.

✍ Only the shallow know themselves.

Had such contradictions been tossed in his face, Wilde would have responded with disdain for the tosser. "Consistency is the last refuge of the unimaginative," he said. Wilde claimed an artist's right to propound a point of view and its obverse, too. In his introduction to "The Truth of Masks," he advised readers, "Not that I agree with everything that I have said in this essay. There is much with which I entirely disagree. . . . For in art there is no such thing as a universal truth. A Truth in art is that whose contradictory is also true."

There was always something of the promising undergraduate about Oscar Wilde: bright, charming, outrageous. Yet the man who could display such insight about others was no more perceptive than the average college sophomore when it came to himself. Biographer Hesketh Pearson thought that the fundamental conflict in Wilde's nature was between his precocious intellect and his immature emotions. Even after he had married and fathered two children, Oscar Wilde's emotional life never progressed much beyond an adolescent's. This could be seen in his lifelong preference for the company of young men. Wilde's unrepentant homosexuality and borderline pederasty challenged the hypocrisy of Victorian sexual attitudes. In Wilde's time and class, the implicit attitude was: Do what you like, but be discreet. Don't flaunt. Wilde flaunted. He was by nature a flaunter. As long as Oscar Wilde wasn't too public about his dalliances, fin de siècle England was willing to look the other way. Only after he rubbed its nose in his passion for young men—and, incidentally, risked pulling the bedsheets off thousands more who shared that passion—did the hammer of British justice fall mercilessly on Wilde's head.

From today's perspective, it's hard to picture how much horror "the love that dare not speak its name" excited in Victorian England. (Had open discussion of the issue been possible, Wilde might have speculated that this was due to the stifled libido of those who were horrified.) Today, Wilde's homosexuality would be a mere peccadillo, no more damning of him than it would later be of Gore Vidal or Edward Albee. Were he still alive, Wilde would be less condemned for being gay, but perhaps taken more to task for exploitation of young men by an older celebrity.

Even as he'd reaped its rewards, Wilde eventually paid the price for being overfamous. His flamboyance and self-promotion made him a household name long before he produced work to merit such recognition. As a result, his fall at the end was that much farther, and harder, accompanied by the delighted applause of the many whom he'd offended in his ostentatious rise to fame. But Wilde didn't take the opportunity to segue from brilliance to profundity after leaving prison. Flashes, hints of what he might have become could be seen in his epic *Ballad of Reading Gaol* and in *De Profundis*, the petulant, sad, and riveting memoir of his life leading to prison. Within *De Profundis*, Wilde continually repeated "the supreme vice is shallowness," as if trying to convince himself. Alas, after his release, Wilde resumed the life of a boulevardier. Now, however, he had neither the resources nor the conviction to do a good job of it. Wilde ended his days as a shabby absinthe drinker in French cafés, cadging francs from old friends and new acquaintances. He couldn't reconceive himself as anything other than brilliantly witty. Yet the thought of returning to drawing-room drama repelled the chastened ex-convict. "I simply have no heart to write clever comedy," he told a friend.

Although outrageous to the end—sipping champagne on his deathbed, remarking that he was dying beyond his means—in later years Wilde did temper his craving to astonish. The post-prison Wilde was in many ways more thoughtful and compassionate than he'd been before his trials. Before, Wilde thought nothing of getting off a good quip at the expense of the destitute. ("If the poor only had profiles there would be no difficulty in solving the problem of poverty.") In prison Wilde developed enormous sympathy for the plight of his fellow convicts. He took particular interest in some rabbit-poaching children who were confined to solitary cells for twenty-three hours of every day. Two letters to a London newspaper denouncing such cruelty were the only pieces of writing Wilde published under his own name during the three and a half years between leaving prison and dying.

It's interesting to speculate how Wilde might have matured with age (a concept he would have loathed). But it's hard to conceive of a gray-haired Oscar Wilde. Not the man who'd spent so many years rapping the aged across their wrinkled knuckles. ("The old should neither be seen nor heard." "Those whom the gods hate die old." "Those whom the gods love grow young.") Wilde venerated youth too much. Like Byron, Capote, and Presley, his appeal was based on brashness. He was far better suited to being an *enfant terrible* than a sage. Oscar Wilde had a good first act and a better second one, but missed the call to his third.

And so we are left with the witty, sometimes wise output of the two productive decades of this writer-raconteur. We all should have such output. It includes not only poetry, fiction, plays, and essays, but stories, repartee, and quips recorded by contemporaries who heard Wilde talk. The challenge confronting anyone who compiles Oscar Wilde's work is to try to convey in print the conversational pyrotechnics that captivated his peers. That's the goal of *The Wit & Wisdom of Oscar Wilde.* Because he was such a master of conversation, it incorporates anecdotes that illustrate his verbal flair. Wilde's gift for thrust and parry is vividly displayed in excerpts from his trial cross-examinations. Sections of Wilde's play scripts showcase both his mastery of witty dialogue and the epigrammatic banter for which Oscar Wilde was famous. The heart of this volume is the best of his sayings—what was known in Wilde's time as "Oscariana." Through his sayings he was known, and through his sayings we shall know him.

Wilde's Wilde

❧ French by sympathy, I am Irish by race, and the English have condemned me to speak the language of Shakespeare.

❧ By nature and by choice, I am extremely indolent.

❧ I am afraid I play no outdoor games at all. Except dominoes. I have sometimes played dominoes outside French cafés.

❧ I never put off till tomorrow what I can possibly do—the day after.

❧ I am never in during the afternoon, except when I am confined to the house by a sharp attack of penury.

❧ I am one of those who are made for exceptions, not for laws.

❧ I have blown my trumpet against the gate of dullness.

❧ I awoke the imagination of my century so that it created myth and legend around me: I summed up all systems in a phrase, and all existence in an epigram.

𝒞𝓋 Praise makes me humble, but when I am abused I know I have touched the stars.

𝒞𝓋 Where will it all end? Half the world does not believe in God, and the other half does not believe in me.

𝒞𝓋 The three women I have most admired are Queen Victoria, Sarah Bernhardt, and Lillie Langtry. I would have married any one of them with pleasure.

𝒞𝓋 While the first editions of most classical authors are those coveted by bibliophiles, it is the second editions of my books that are the true rarities.

𝒞𝓋 If I were all alone, marooned on some desert island and had my things with me, I should dress for dinner every evening.

𝒞𝓋 I have the simplest tastes. I am always satisfied with the best.

𝒞𝓋 Between me and life there is a mist of words always.

𝒞𝓋 I like to do all the talking myself. It saves time and prevents arguments.

𝒞𝓋 I like hearing myself talk. It is one of my greatest pleasures. I often have long conversations all by myself, and I am so clever that sometimes I don't understand a single word of what I am saying.

𝒞𝓋 Geniuses . . . are always talking about themselves, when I want them to be thinking about me.

𝒞𝓋 I am always thinking about myself, and I expect everybody else to do the same.

❧ If life be, as it surely is, a problem to me, I am no less a problem to life.

❧ I filled my life to the very brim with pleasure, as one might fill a cup to the very brim with wine.

❧ Whatever my life may have been ethically, it has always been *romantic*.

❧ My record of perversities of passion and distorted romances would fill many scarlet volumes.

❧ God would grow weary if I told my sins.

❧ I must say . . . that I ruined myself: and that nobody, great or small, can be ruined except by his own hand.

❧ A patriot put in prison for loving his country loves his country, and a poet in prison for loving boys loves boys. To have altered my life would have been to have admitted that Uranian love is ignoble. I hold it to be noble, more noble than other forms.

❧ I entered prison with a heart of stone, thinking only of my pleasure, but now my heart has been broken; pity has entered my heart; I now understand that pity is the greatest and the most beautiful thing that there is in the world. And that's why I can't be angry with those who condemned me, nor with anyone, because then I would not have known all that.

❧ I am not a scrap ashamed of having been in prison. I am horribly ashamed of the materialism of the life that brought me there. It was quite unworthy of an artist.

The Anecdotal Wilde

FULL NAME

Oscar and Wilde weren't the only names bequeathed him by his Irish parents. "I started as Oscar Fingal O'Flahertie Wills Wilde," he once said. "All but two of the five names have already been thrown overboard. Soon I shall discard another and be known simply as 'The Wilde' or 'The Oscar.'"

SUSPENSE

In Wilde's time, Oxford applicants had to translate biblical passages aloud from Greek. Assigned one dealing with the Passion, Wilde began translating with ease. His examiners said he could stop. Wilde continued. When the examiners finally got the young Dubliner to pause, he said, "Oh, do let me go on. I want to see how it ends."

LIKE MOTHER

Wilde's mother was a statuesque woman of unconventional views and a lofty contempt for respectability. Her son once invited an

Oxford classmate to visit him at his mother's, "where we have founded a Society for the Suppression of Virtue."

HIGH STANDARDS

Oscar Wilde first appeared in England's national conversation while still at Oxford. According to a story that swept the country, several fellow students found Wilde staring raptly at a pair of blue vases on his mantelpiece. Asked what he was doing, Wilde replied, "I am trying to live up to my china." This quip was applauded by some for its wit, denounced by others for its irreverence.

FAME

Not long af er leaving Oxford, Wilde walked with a friend outside a London theater. Both heard a passerby remark, "There goes that bloody fool Oscar Wilde."

"It's extraordinary how soon one gets known in London," observed Wilde.

PATH TO THE STARS

Wilde's postgraduate notoriety was due in no small part to being parodied as a flower-loving poet in Gilbert and Sullivan's *Patience*. One song in that comic opera included the lyrics

Though the Philistines may jostle,
You will rank as an apostle
In the high aesthetic band,
If you walk down Piccadilly
With a poppy or a lily
In your medieval hand.

Although Wilde denied that he'd ever strolled about London clutching a poppy or lily, the assumption that he did only added to his renown. "Anyone could have done that," he explained of the ambulatory flower worship attributed to him. "The great and difficult thing was what I achieved—to make the whole world believe that I had done it."

ALTRUISM

William Gilbert (of Gilbert and Sullivan) met Wilde at a dinner party. As usual, Wilde dominated the gathering with his stories and wit. "I wish I could talk like you," said Gilbert during a rare pause. "I'd keep my mouth shut and claim it as a virtue!"

"Ah, that would be selfish," responded Wilde. "I could deny myself the pleasure of talking, but not to others the pleasure of listening."

GOD SAVE THE QUEEN

Wilde claimed that he could discuss any subject at any time, prepared or not. Taking him up on this claim, a companion asked for his views on the subject of the queen. Responded Wilde: "The queen is not a subject."

TOUCHÉ

Now and again Wilde found himself bested at banter. One such occasion took place in America, where a woman told him something was "awfully nice."

"But 'nice' is such a nasty word," said a bored-looking Wilde.

"Really, Mr. Wilde?" she responded. "But is 'nasty' such a nice word?"

HARD OF HEARING

Wilde watched one of his Oxford professors give a lecture in London. The man was painfully soft-spoken. Afterward, he asked some members of the audience if they'd heard him. "Overheard now and then," said Wilde.

LITERARY WORSHIP

During a literary gathering at London's Café Royal, talk turned to Richard Le Gallienne's book *The Religion of a Literary Man.* A publisher present blasted this poet for presuming to subject readers to his views on religion. "My dear fellow," said Wilde, "of course Le Gallienne is quite right. How far you are behind the times! Surely you know that nowadays the religion of a literary man is an affair strictly between himself . . . and his public."

HURT FEELINGS

Wilde told Le Gallienne that he had a bone to pick with him. He'd read *The Religion of a Literary Man,* Wilde explained, and thought Le Gallienne had treated him poorly within. "Most unkind," he said. "I could not believe it of you—so unkind to so true a friend."

"Why, I can't remember that I even mentioned your name in it," responded a puzzled Le Gallienne.

"Ah!" said Wilde. "Richard, that was just it."

GOOD MANNERS

Wilde joined a friend for an evening at a music hall. Part of the program consisted of a mimic, who announced the subject of each impersonation before performing it. "Perfectly splendid," Wilde said afterward of this man's performance. "And I do think it so kind of him to tell us who he is imitating. It avoids discussion, doesn't it."

ECONOMY

Someone suggested to Wilde that all dramatic critics could be bought. "Judging from their appearance, most of them cannot be at all expensive," he responded. This remark later showed up in *The Picture of Dorian Gray*.

FAVORITE TOPIC

Punch published a fanciful conversation about actresses between Wilde and James McNeill Whistler, who at the time were best of friends. In response, Wilde wired Whistler, "*Punch* too ridiculous. When you and I are together we never talk about anything except *ourselves*."

Whistler wired back, "No, no, Oscar, you forget. When you and I are together, we never talk about anything except *me*."

"It is true, Jimmy," Wilde is said to have responded, "we were talking about you, but I was thinking of myself."

ELOCUTION

Before leaving London for his 1882 lecture tour of America, Wilde took elocution lessons from a friend. "I want a natural style," Wilde told his teacher, "with a touch of affectation."

"Well," said the teacher, "and haven't you got that, Oscar?"

CUSTOMS DECLARATION

After Wilde landed in New York, a customs official asked what he had to declare. "Nothing but my genius," replied Wilde.

DISAPPOINTMENT I

A fellow passenger told American reporters that Wilde hadn't been pleased with the Atlantic. "It is not so majestic as I expected," he'd explained. "The roaring ocean doesn't roar." Subsequent headlines—MR. WILDE DISAPPOINTED WITH THE ATLANTIC—only added to his reputation for being blasé.

DISAPPOINTMENT II

Like the Atlantic, Niagara Falls didn't live up to Wilde's expectations. He found the falls "wanting in grandeur and variety of line." All they were, he thought, was "a vast unnecessary amount of water going the wrong way and then falling over unnecessary rocks." Wilde characterized tourists visiting Niagara as "melancholy people, who wandered about trying to get up that feeling of sublimity which the guidebooks assured them they could do without extra charge." He later added, "Every American bride is taken there, and the sight of the stupendous waterfall must be one of the earliest, if not the keenest, disappointments in American married life."

WEATHER FORECAST

An English newspaper reported that Wilde had been spotted on a clear day in Boston wearing a mackintosh and carrying an umbrella. When asked why, he'd responded, "I hear that it is raining in London this morning." Wilde's friend Robert Sherard asked him if the story was true. Wilde termed it "a false report."

"Ah, I thought so," said Sherard.

"Yes," continued Wilde, "I discovered later that the weather had been perfect in London that day."

ROYAL REBUKE

When Wilde met Henry Wadsworth Longfellow in Boston, the older poet told him of meeting Queen Victoria at Windsor Castle some years earlier. Longfellow told her he was surprised to find himself so widely read in England. The queen corroborated that the American poet was well-known among her subjects. "All my servants read you," she told him. Longfellow said that he sometimes lay awake at night wondering if this comment was meant as a slight. Wilde assured him that it was, that it was Majesty's rebuke to the vanity of the poet.

HEAVENLY

At a reception in Cincinnati, Wilde urged the hostess to publish her poetry. "Perhaps," she responded, "in heaven, instead of holding receptions, I may get out a book."

"No, no," said Wilde. "There'll be no publishers there."

UNDERWHELMED

Wilde was not taken with Cincinnati. "I wonder your criminals don't plead the ugliness of your city as an excuse for their crimes," he told a reporter. St. Louis didn't impress him any better. "Several St. Louis citizens told me the city was not at its best," Wilde remarked. "I should have thought so, even though the information was lacking."

ON SECOND THOUGHT

In his lectures on aestheticism, Wilde said that pictures should be hung at eye level. "The habit in America of hanging them up near the cornice struck me as irrational at first," he observed. "It was not until I saw how bad the pictures were that I realized the advantage of the custom."

WILDE'S WEST

Wilde was warned to avoid Leadville, Colorado, whose pistol-packing residents would surely shoot him or his traveling manager. Wilde said he wrote ahead to tell Leadvillians that nothing they could do to his traveling manager would intimidate him.

In a Leadville saloon he was charmed by a sign reading PLEASE DO NOT SHOOT THE PIANIST. HE IS DOING HIS BEST. Wilde called this "the only rational method of art criticism I have ever come across." At his lecture in Leadville, Wilde later wrote, a depiction of the early Florentines failed to elicit any response from his audience of miners. But when he described one of Whistler's artistic crimes, "Then they leaped to their feet and in their grand simple style swore that such things should not be. Some of the younger ones pulled their revolvers out and left hurriedly to see if Jimmy was 'prowling about the saloons' or 'wrestling a hash' at any eating shop."

Wilde later descended by bucket into a mine shaft, where he used a silver drill to open a new vein of silver dubbed "The Oscar." "I had hoped that in their simple way they would have offered me shares in 'The Oscar,'" he wrote a friend, "but in their artless untutored fashion they did not."

POSTWAR BLUES

One of Wilde's favorite anecdotes about America involved those southern states whose older citizens dated important events from the

Civil War. "How beautiful the moon is tonight," Wilde said he'd remarked to a Southerner.

"Yes," the Southerner replied, "but you should have seen it before the war."

In some of Wilde's retellings, the maker of this remark was a woman, in others a man. The comment's real author was probably Oscar Wilde.

SIGNS OF SUCCESS

At the end of his lecture tour, Wilde developed a stock response for those who asked how it had gone. "A great success!" he'd tell them. "I had two secretaries, one to answer my letters, the other to send locks of hair to my admirers. I have had to let them both go, poor fellows: one is in hospital with writer's cramp, and the other is quite bald."

ARTISTIC INTEGRITY

Wilde lingered in New York, hoping someone there might produce his play *Vera*. When a theater manager offered him an advance on condition he make certain changes in his script, its author demurred. "Who am I to tamper with a masterpiece?" he asked. (Wilde liked this line so much that he repeated it often, with regard to requested changes in subsequent plays.)

LOCATION, LOCATION

When Wilde spent a few months in Paris, Robert Sherard visited him there, in his apartment overlooking the Seine. Peering out the window, Sherard commented on the beauty of the view. Wilde told him that the view mattered only to the innkeeper, who added it to his bill. Besides, he added, "A gentleman never looks out the window."

RISK

As Wilde and some friends toured a dubious section of Paris one evening, Sherard proclaimed loudly that whoever dared meddle with his friend Oscar Wilde would be sorry. "Sherard," Wilde interjected, "you are defending us at the risk of our lives."

WILDLY BOURGEOIS

The French actor Coquelin invited Oscar Wilde to visit him at home. Wilde asked when he'd be there.

"I am always at home about nine o' clock," said Coquelin.

"Very well. Then I shall come one evening."

"But, Monsieur, it is at nine o'clock in the morning that I meant."

"Oh, Monsieur Coquelin," said Wilde, who routinely slept until midday, "you are a remarkable man indeed. I am much more bourgeois than you are. I always go to bed about four or five o'clock. I have never been able to stay awake until *that* hour."

SELF-ESTEEM

Wilde watched a well-known French poet make a scene at a banquet because he hadn't been seated at the head table. Wilde was struck by the absurdity of this protest. "Could anything be more petty," he asked, "a greater revelation of insignificance? Now for me, the highest place is where I am myself."

THE TAXMAN COMETH

A stranger accosted Wilde one afternoon in front of his London home.

"I have called about the taxes," said this man.

"Taxes!" responded Wilde. "Why should I pay taxes?"

"But, sir, you are the householder here, are you not? You live here, you sleep here."

"Ah, yes; but then, you see, I sleep so badly."

DOMESTIC TRAGEDY

While visiting him at home, a friend watched one of Wilde's two sons address him as "my good papa." Wilde patted the boy and said, "Don't call me that. It sounds so respectable."

PRAYERS

Wilde couldn't get his son Cyril to ask God to make him good. He didn't *want* to be good, said the obstinate boy. Why pray for something he didn't want? When Wilde pressed the point, Cyril suggested an alternative: he'd ask God to make his baby brother good. Wilde loved recounting this story. He thought it made perfectly the point that we'd much rather reform others than ourselves.

BEDEVILMENT

To illustrate his contention that the hardest thing to bear was a friend's good fortune, Wilde told Arthur Conan Doyle this story: "The devil was once crossing the Libyan Desert, and he came upon a spot where a number of small fiends were tormenting a holy hermit. The sainted man easily shook off their evil suggestions. The devil watched their failure and then he stepped forward to give them a lesson. 'What you do is too crude,' said he. 'Permit me for one moment.' With that he whispered to the holy man, 'Your brother has just been made Bishop of Alexandria.' A scowl of malignant jealousy at once clouded the serene face of the hermit. 'That,' said the devil to his imps, 'is the sort of thing which I should recommend.'"

PLAGIARISM

A woman once told Wilde that a key episode in one of his plays reminded her of a scene in one written by Augustin-Eugène Scribe. "Taken bodily from it, dear lady," admitted Wilde. "Why not? Nobody reads nowadays."

SECRET SOCIETY

Wilde asked several friends to each wear a green carnation during opening night of *Lady Windermere's Fan* (having discovered a florist who produced this unlikely flower, probably with the help of dye). "I want a good many men to wear them tomorrow," he explained. "It will annoy the public."

"But why annoy the public?" asked one of the men.

"It likes to be annoyed," said Wilde. "A young man on the stage will wear a green carnation; people will stare at it and wonder. Then they will look round the house and see here and there more and more specks of mystic green. 'This must be some secret symbol,' they will say; 'what on earth can it mean?'"

"And what does it mean?'"

"Nothing whatever, but that is just what nobody will guess."

RECIPE FOR SUCCESS

As *The Importance of Being Earnest* was about to open, a reporter asked Wilde if he expected the play to be a success. "My dear fellow," Wilde responded, "you have got it wrong. The play *is* a success. The only question is whether the first night's audience will be one."

UNCANNY RESEMBLANCE

The first night's audience gave *The Importance of Being Earnest* an extended standing ovation. Afterward, theater manager George Alexander asked Wilde how he liked the production. "My dear Alec," he responded, "it was charming, quite charming. And, do you know, from time to time I was reminded of a play I once wrote myself called *The Importance of Being Earnest.*"

BEST BOOKS

Wilde was asked to name the one hundred best all-time books. "I fear that would be impossible," he responded. And why was that? "Because I have written only five."

SANITY

After being told of psychiatrist Max Nordau's conviction that geniuses were mad, Wilde responded, "I quite agree with Dr. Nordau's assertion that all men of genius are insane, but Dr. Nordau forgets that all sane people are idiots."

POPULARITY

During a Café Royal gathering, Frank Harris boasted of the many London homes to which he'd been invited. "Yes, dear Frank, we believe you," observed Wilde. "You have dined in every house in London, *once.*"

YANKEE GO HOME

After being introduced to Richard Harding Davis, Wilde noted that the American journalist was from Philadelphia, where Washington was buried. Davis pointed out that Washington was buried in Mount Vernon, Virginia. Wilde did not appreciate being corrected. He changed the subject—to a new French painter. "Do let's hear what Mr. Davis thinks of him," he told the group surrounding them. "Americans always talk so amusingly of art."

"I never talk about things when I don't know the facts," said Davis.

"That must limit your conversation frightfully," said Wilde.

FAMILIARITY BREEDS CONTEMPT

A man greeted Wilde by saying "Hello, Oscar!" while slapping him on the shoulder.

"I don't know you by sight," Wilde told the shoulder-slapper, "but your manner is familiar."

GAG ORDER

Wilde greeted a late arrival to a reception with the words, "Oh, I'm so glad you've come! There are a hundred things I want not to say to you."

GOOD VALUE

Lord Alfred Douglas left a love letter from Wilde in the pocket of a suit he gave away. Eventually a blackmailer appeared on Wilde's doorstep asking if he might like to buy it back. "A very curious construction can be put on that letter," the blackmailer warned the playwright.

"Art is rarely intelligible to the criminal classes," observed Wilde.

"A man has offered me sixty pounds for it," the blackmailer continued.

"If you take my advice you will go to that man and sell my letter to him for sixty pounds," advised Wilde. "I myself have never received so large a sum for any prose work of that length; but I am glad to find that there is someone in England who considers a letter of mine worth sixty pounds."

For ten shillings Wilde recovered possession of the letter.

HARD LABOR

Wilde told a hostess that he'd toiled strenuously all day long. "I was working on the proof of one of my poems all the morning and took out a comma," he said.

"And in the afternoon?" asked his host.

"In the afternoon—well, I put it back again."

HOUSEHOLD NAME

During his trials, Wilde's name dominated London newspapers and their advertising placards. "Well," suggested Robert Sherard as they passed such a placard, "you have got your name before the public at last."

"Nobody can pretend now not to have heard of it," agreed Wilde with a rueful laugh.

ROYAL TREATMENT

After his imprisonment, Wilde was returned to court on bankruptcy charges. While being transported he was made to stand outside in the rain, handcuffed to two other prisoners. "Sir," England's most famous convict told a prison official accompanying them, "if this is the way Queen Victoria treats her convicts she doesn't deserve to have any."

TACTLESSNESS

Toward the end of his two-year sentence, a prison official informed Wilde that his aunt had died. He then added that it might interest him to know that Sir Edward Poynter, a minor artist, had been elected president of the Royal Academy. "I am grateful to you for your kindness in telling me about my poor aunt," responded Wilde, "but perhaps you might have broken Poynter to me more gently."

KINDNESS

After his release, Wilde went to Dieppe on the northern coast of France. A friend wondered what a man who was lurking about Wilde's rented chalet might be up to. "I fancy he is a detective in the pay of Queensberry," said Wilde, referring to Lord Alfred Douglas's father, the Marquis of Queensberry, who had hounded him into prison. "I am sorry for him. It must be tedious work. I have sometimes thought of talking to him and trying to cheer him up, for he has a sad countenance; but then, you see, the romance of secrecy would be gone, and I am sure he has nothing else to live for."

REDEMPTION

At the urging of his friend Ernest Dowson, Wilde consented to have a go with a Dieppe prostitute. This was his first heterosexual contact in more than a decade. The experiment was not a success. Wilde later compared their coupling to chewing cold mutton. "But tell it in England," he advised Dowson of this episode, "where it will entirely restore my reputation."

LAST WORDS

It would seem only fitting for one of history's greatest wits to exit with a quip. By legend this did happen. Oscar Wilde's putative last quip varies, however. Some think that before expiring Wilde said that he was dying as he lived, beyond his means. The playwright did say this, but it was several days before the end. In other recountings Wilde murmured "Either the wallpaper goes or I go," then went. In fact, well before the end Wilde told a visitor to his tacky hotel room, "My wallpaper and I are fighting a duel to the death. One or the other of us has to go."

Wilde's friend Robert Ross was present at his death. According to Ross, after spending a few hours in a silent semi-coma Wilde heaved a deep sigh and died.

Oscariana

ACTING

    ✍ I love acting. It is so much more real than life.

    ✍ Why should not degrees be granted for good acting? Are they not given to those who misunderstand Plato and who mistranslate Aristotle?

    ✍ Anybody can act. Most people in England do nothing else.

AGE

    ✍ Men become old, but they never become good.

    ✍ The old should neither be seen nor heard.

    ✍ I always contradict the aged; I do it on principle.

    ✍ As soon as people are old enough to know better, they don't know anything at all.

↫ Those whom the gods hate die old.

↫ Those whom the gods love grow young.

↫ Young men want to be faithful, and are not; old men want to be faithless, and cannot.

↫ The old believe everything; the middle-aged suspect everything; the young know everything.

↫ The tragedy of old age is not that one is old, but that one is young.

↫ The secret of remaining young is never to have an emotion that is unbecoming.

↫ Youth smiles without any reason. It is one of its chiefest charms.

↫ It's absurd to talk of the ignorance of youth. The only people to whose opinions I listen now with any respect are persons much younger than myself. They seem in front of me. Life has revealed to them her latest wonder.

↫ I have never learned anything except from people younger than myself.

↫ We never get back our youth. The pulse of joy that beats in us at twenty, becomes sluggish. Our limbs fail, our senses rot. We degenerate into hideous puppets, haunted by the memory of the passions of which we were too much afraid, and the exquisite temptations that we had not the courage to yield to.

To get back one's youth one has merely to repeat one's follies.

To get back my youth I would do anything in the world, except take exercise, get up early, or be respectable.

ALTRUISM

The majority of men spoil their lives by an exaggerated and unhealthy altruism.

The desire to do good to others produces a plentiful supply of prigs.

One can always be kind to people about whom one cares nothing.

Conscience and cowardice are really the same things. Conscience is the trade name of the firm.

The mere existence of conscience . . . is a sign of our imperfect development. It must be merged with instinct before we become fine. Self-denial is simply a method by which man arrests his progress, and self-sacrifice a survival of the mutilation of the savage, part of that old worship of pain which is so terrible a factor in the history of the world.

Self-sacrifice is a thing that should be put down by law. It is so demoralizing to the people for whom one sacrifices oneself.

Good intentions have been the ruin of the world. The only

people who have achieved anything have been those who have had no intentions at all.

    ⚭ Whenever a man does a thoroughly stupid thing, it is always from the noblest motives.

    ⚭ It takes a thoroughly good woman to do a thoroughly stupid thing.

    ⚭ Philanthropy seems to me to have become simply the refuge of people who wish to annoy their fellow creatures.

    ⚭ Philanthropic people lose all sense of humanity. It is their distinguishing characteristic.

    ⚭ People are so fond of giving away what they do not want themselves, that charity is largely on the increase.

    ⚭ Charity creates a multitude of sins.

AMERICA

    ⚭ English people are far more interested in American barbarism than they are in American civilization.

    ⚭ We have really everything in common with America nowadays, except, of course, language.

    ⚭ America has never quite forgiven Europe for having been discovered somewhat earlier in history than itself.

    ⚭ It is a vulgar error to suppose that America was ever discovered. It was merely detected.

❧ America is one long expectoration.

❧ America is the noisiest country that ever existed.

❧ One is impressed in America, but not favorably impressed, by the inordinate size of everything. The country seems to try to bully one into a belief in its power by its impressive bigness.

❧ Bulk is their canon of beauty and size their standard of excellence.

❧ Everybody seems in a hurry to catch a train. This is a state of things which is not favorable to poetry or romance. Had Romeo or Juliet been in a constant state of anxiety about trains, or had their minds been agitated by the question of return tickets, Shakespeare could not have given us those lovely balcony scenes.

❧ I am told that pork-packing is the most lucrative profession in America, after politics.

❧ The people of America understand money-making, but not how to spend it.

❧ In America the President reigns for four years, and Journalism governs forever and ever.

❧ In America the young are always ready to give those who are older than themselves the full benefits of their inexperience.

❧ The American child educates its father and mother.

❧ There at any rate is a country that has no trappings, no pageantry, and no gorgeous ceremonies. I saw only two processions—one was the Fire Brigade preceded by the Police, the other was the Police preceded by the Fire Brigade.

 ✑ In America there is no opening for a fool. They expect brains, even from a bootblack, and get them.

 ✑ In going to America one learns that poverty is not a necessary accompaniment to civilization.

 ✑ It is impossible not to think nobly of a country that has produced Patrick Henry, Thomas Jefferson, George Washington, and Jefferson Davis.

 ✑ The Americans are the best politically educated people in the world. It is well worth one's while to go to a country which can teach us the beauty of the word FREEDOM and the value of the thing LIBERTY.

AMERICANS

 ✑ All Americans lecture, I believe. I suppose it is something in their climate.

 ✑ The American woman is the most decorated and decorative object I have seen in America.

 ✑ Many American ladies on leaving their native land adopt an appearance of chronic ill-health, under the impression that it is a form of European refinement.

 ✑ American girls are pretty and charming—little oases of pretty unreasonableness in a vast desert of practical common sense.

American women are bright, clever, and wonderfully cosmopolitan. Their patriotic feelings are limited to an admiration for Niagara and a regret for the Elevated Railway; and, unlike the men, they never bore us with Bunkers Hill.

For him [the American man] Art has no marvel, and Beauty no meaning, and the Past no message. He thinks that civilization began with the introduction of steam, and looks with contempt upon all centuries that had no hot-water apparatuses in their houses.

The telephone is his test of civilization, and his wildest dreams of Utopia do not rise beyond elevated railways and electric bells.

Real experience comes to them so much sooner than it does to us that they are never awkward, never shy, and never say foolish things except when they ask one how the Hudson River compares with the Rhine, or whether Brooklyn Bridge is not really more impressive than the dome at St. Paul's.

The American man marries early, and the American woman marries often, and they get on extremely well together.

If the Americans are not the most well-dressed people in the world, they are the most comfortably dressed.

APPAREL

A man is called affected, nowadays, if he dresses as he likes to dress. But in doing that he is acting in a perfectly natural manner. Affectation, in such matters, consists in dressing according to the views of one's neighbor, whose views, as they are the views of the majority, will probably be extremely stupid.

  Every right article of apparel belongs equally to both sexes, and there is absolutely no such thing as a definitely feminine garment.

  All costumes are caricatures.

  Cavaliers and Puritans are interesting for their costumes, not their convictions.

  The artistic feeling of a nation should find expression in its costume quite as much as in its architecture.

  One should either be a work of art, or wear a work of art.

  The only way to atone for being occasionally a little over-dressed is by being always absolutely over-educated.

  The imagination will concentrate itself on the waistcoat. Waistcoats will show whether a man can admire poetry or not.

  It is really only the idle classes who dress badly. Wherever physical labor of any kind is required, the costume used is, as a rule, absolutely right, for labor necessitates freedom, and without freedom there is no such thing as beauty in dress at all.

  Tails have no place in costume, except on some Darwinian theory of heredity.

  With an evening coat and a white tie, anybody, even a stockbroker, can gain a reputation for being civilized.

APPEARANCES

 ∗ It is only shallow people who do not judge by appearances.

 ∗ Being natural is simply a pose, and the most irritating pose I know.

 ∗ Perhaps one never seems so much at one's ease as when one has to play a part.

 ∗ Man is least himself when he talks in his own person. Give him a mask, and he will tell you the truth.

 ∗ A mask tells us more than a face.

 ∗ The truth about the life of a man is not what he does, but the legend which he creates around himself.

 ∗ I think a man should invent his own myth.

ART

 ∗ Art is not something which you can take or leave. It is a necessity of human life.

 ∗ Art is the mathematical result of the emotional desire for beauty.

 ∗ It is through Art, and through Art only, that we can realize our perfection; through Art, and through Art only, that we can shield ourselves from the sordid perils of actual existence.

 ∗ Art is what makes the life of each citizen a sacrament and not a speculation.

✐ The secret of life is in art.

✐ Life imitates Art far more than Art imitates Life.

✐ It is the spectator, and not life, that art really mirrors.

✐ The work of art is to dominate the spectator: the spectator is not to dominate the work of art. The spectator is to be receptive. He is to be the violin on which the master is to play. And the more completely he can suppress his own silly views, his own foolish prejudices, his own absurd ideas of what Art should be, the more likely he is to understand and appreciate the work of art in question.

✐ The meaning of any beautiful created thing is, at least, as much in the soul of him who looks at it, as it was in his soul who wrought it.

✐ That is the mission of true art—to make us pause and look at a thing a second time.

✐ To reveal art and conceal the artist is art's aim.

✐ The aim of art is no more to give pleasure than to give pain. The aim of art is to be art.

✐ There are works which wait, and which one does not understand for a long time; the reason is that they bring answers to questions which have not yet been raised; for the question often arrives a terribly long time after the answer.

✐ There is no mood or passion that Art cannot give us, and those of us who have discovered her secret can settle beforehand what our experience is going to be. We can choose our day and select our hour.

☙ Art is the one thing which death cannot harm.

☙ All good work looks perfectly modern: a piece of Greek sculpture, a portrait of Velázquez—they are always modern, always of our time.

☙ The public make use of the classics of a country as a means of checking the progress of Art. They degrade the classics into authorities. They use them as bludgeons for preventing the free expression of Beauty in new forms.

☙ The one thing that the public dislike is novelty. Any attempt to extend the subject matter of art is extremely distasteful to the public.

☙ A fresh mode of Beauty is absolutely distasteful to them [the public], and whenever it appears they get so angry and bewildered that they always use two stupid expressions—one is that the work of art is grossly unintelligible; the other, that the work of art is grossly immoral.

☙ Popularity is the crown of laurel which the world puts on bad art.

☙ No art is better than bad art.

☙ It is very curious the connection between Faith and bad art: I feel it myself.

☙ All bad art is the result of good intentions.

It is always with the best intentions that the worst work is done.

The best that one can say of most modern creative art is that it is just a little less vulgar than reality.

All art is quite useless.

All art is immoral.

Art must be loved for its own sake, and not criticized by a standard of morality.

The sign of a Philistine age is the cry of immorality against art.

No art ever survived censorship; no art ever will.

Whenever a community or a powerful section of a community, or a government of any kind, attempts to dictate to the artist what he is to do, Art either entirely vanishes, or becomes stereotyped, or degenerates into a low and ignoble form of craft.

There are two ways of disliking art. . . . One is to dislike it. The other is to like it rationally.

It is only an auctioneer who can equally and impartially admire all schools of Art.

Diversity of opinion about a work of art shows that the work is new, complex, and vital.

Art should always remain mysterious. Artists, like Gods, must never leave their pedestals.

ARTISTS

   Cͽ Artists, like the Greek gods, are revealed only to one another.

   Cͽ A really great artist can never judge of other people's work at all, and can hardly, in fact, judge of his own. That very concentration of vision that makes a man an artist, limits by its sheer intensity his faculty of fine appreciation. The energy of creation hurries him blindly on to his own goal. The wheels of his chariot raise the dust of a cloud around him. The gods are hidden from each other. They recognize only their worshipers.

   Cͽ The moment that an artist takes notice of what other people want, and tries to supply the demand, he ceases to be an artist, and becomes a dull or an amusing craftsman, an honest or a dishonest tradesman.

   Cͽ Alone, without any reference to his neighbors, without any interference the artist can fashion a beautiful thing; and if he does not do it solely for his own pleasure, he is not an artist at all.

   Cͽ Creation for the joy of creation is the aim of the artist, and that is why the artist is a more divine type than the saint.

   Cͽ When critics disagree the artist is in accord with himself.

   Cͽ The true artist is a man who believes absolutely in himself, because he is absolutely himself.

   Cͽ Bad artists always admire each other's work. They call it being large-minded and free from prejudice. But a truly great artist cannot conceive of life being shown, or beauty fashioned, under any conditions other than those that he has selected.

✒ A true artist takes no notice whatever of the public. The public to him are nonexistent.

✒ Most of our modern portrait painters are doomed to absolute oblivion. They never paint what they see. They paint what the public sees, and the public never sees anything.

✒ The only thing that the artist cannot see is the obvious. The only thing that the public can see is the obvious.

✒ The more the public is interested in artists, the less it is interested in art. The personality of the artist is not a thing the public should know anything about.

✒ The English public, as usual hypocritical, prudish, and philistine, has not known how to find the art in the work of art; it has searched for the man in it. Since it always confuses the man and his creations, it thinks that to create Hamlet you must be a little melancholy, to imagine Lear completely mad.

✒ To call an artist morbid because he deals with morbidity as his subject matter is as silly as if one called Shakespeare mad because he wrote *King Lear*.

✒ How can a man who regards success as a goal of life be a true artist?

✒ No artist desires to prove anything. Even things that are true can be proved.

✒ No artist has ethical sympathies. An ethical sympathy in an artist is an unpardonable mannerism of style.

❧ Insincerity and treachery . . . somehow seem inseparable from the artistic temperament.

❧ Vice and virtue are to the artist materials for an art.

❧ The young artist who paints nothing but beautiful things . . . misses one half of the world.

❧ Nothing . . . is more dangerous to the young artist than any conception of ideal beauty: he is constantly led by it either into weak prettiness or lifeless abstraction.

❧ No great artist ever sees things as they really are. If he did, he would cease to be an artist.

❧ The greatest artists are stupid and tiresome men as a rule.

❧ The only artists I have ever known who are personally delightful are bad artists. Good artists exist simply in what they make, and consequently are perfectly uninteresting in what they are.

❧ Only mediocrities progress. An artist revolves in a cycle of masterpieces, the first of which is no less perfect than the last.

❧ In New York, and even in Boston, a good model is so great a rarity that most of the artists are reduced to painting Niagara and millionaires.

❧ For an artist to marry his model is as fatal as for a gourmet to marry his cook; the one gets no sittings, the other no dinners.

BEATY

ఈ The desire for beauty is merely a heightened form of the desire for life.

ఈ When the result is beautiful, the method is justified.

ఈ The best service of God is found in the worship of all that is beautiful.

ఈ Beauty, like Wisdom, loves the lonely worshiper.

ఈ Those who do not love beauty more than truth never know the inmost shrine of art.

ఈ Devotion to beauty and to the creation of beautiful things is the test of all great civilized nations.

ఈ Beauty is a form of Genius—is higher indeed, than Genius, as it needs no explanation.

ఈ Beauty has as many meanings as man has moods.

ఈ Philosophies fall away like sand, and creeds follow one another like the withered leaves of autumn; but what is beautiful is a joy for all seasons and a possession for all eternity.

ఈ All beautiful things belong to the same age.

ఈ Beauty is the only thing that time cannot harm.

ఈ No object is so ugly that, under certain conditions of light and shade, or proximity to other things, it will not look beautiful; no object is so beautiful that, under certain conditions, it will not look ugly. I believe that in every twenty-four hours what is beautiful looks ugly, and what is ugly looks beautiful, once.

✍ I have found that all ugly things are made by those who strive to make something beautiful, and that all beautiful things are made by those who strive to make something useful.

✍ Utility will be always on the side of the beautiful things.

✍ Good machinery is graceful . . . the line of strength and the line of beauty being one.

✍ The reason we love the lily and the sunflower, in spite of what Mr. Gilbert may tell you, is not for any vegetable fashion at all. It is because these two lovely flowers are in England the two most perfect models of design.

✍ Aestheticism is a search after the signs of the beautiful . . . It is, to speak more exactly, the search after the secret of life.

✍ Aesthetics, like sexual selection, make life lovely and wonderful, fill it with new forms, and give it progress, and variety and change.

✍ Aesthetics are higher than ethics. They belong to a more spiritual sphere. To discern the beauty of a thing is the finest point to which one can arrive.

✍ Even a color-sense is more important, in the development of the individual, than a sense of right and wrong.

CLASS

✍ It is only by not paying one's bills that one can hope to live in the memory of the commercial classes.

✍ If the lower orders don't set us a good example, what on earth is the use of them? They seem, as a class, to have absolutely no sense of moral responsibility.

✍ Each class preaches the importance of those virtues it need not exercise. The rich harp on the value of thrift, the idle grow eloquent over the dignity of labor.

✍ There is only one class in the community that thinks more about money than the rich, and that is the poor.

✍ Extravagance is the luxury of the poor, penury the luxury of the rich.

✍ As for the virtuous poor, one can pity them, of course, but one cannot possibly admire them.

✍ We are often told that the poor are grateful for charity. Some of them are, no doubt, but the best amongst the poor are never grateful. They are ungrateful, discontented, disobedient, and rebellious. They are quite right to be so.

✍ To recommend thrift to the poor is both grotesque and insulting. It is like advising a man who is starving to eat less.

✍ Why should they [the poor] be grateful for the crumbs that fall from the rich man's table? They should be seated at the board, and are beginning to know it.

The real tragedy of the poor is that they can afford nothing but self-denial. Beautiful sins, like beautiful things, are the privilege of the rich.

The poor are wiser, more charitable, more kind, more sensitive than we are.

I quite sympathize with the rage of the English democracy against what they call the vices of the upper orders. The masses feel that drunkenness, stupidity, and immorality should be their own special property, and that if any one of us makes an ass of himself he is poaching on their preserves.

Those who have much are often greedy. Those who have little always share.

A *grande passion* is the privilege of people who have nothing to do. That is the one use of the idle classes of a country.

There is always more brass than brains in an aristocracy.

Study the Peerage. . . . It is the one book a young man about town should know thoroughly, and it is the best thing in fiction the English have ever done.

COMMON SENSE

The inherited stupidity of the race—sound English common sense.

The growth of common sense in the English Church is a thing very much to be regretted.

  Common sense is the enemy of romance.

  Anybody can have common sense, provided that they have no imagination.

  I love superstitions. They are the color element of thought and imagination. They are the opponents of common sense.

  Nowadays most people die of a sort of creeping common sense, and discover, when it is too late, that the only thing one never regrets are one's mistakes.

CONFORMITY

  While to the claims of charity a man may yield and yet be free, to the claims of conformity no man may yield and remain free at all.

  People . . . go through their lives in a sort of coarse comfort, like petted animals, without ever realizing that they are probably thinking other people's thoughts, living by other people's standards, wearing practically what one may call other people's second-hand clothes, and never being themselves for a single moment.

  Most people are other people. Their thoughts are someone else's opinions, their lives a mimicry, their passions a quotation.

  Selfishness is not living as one wishes to live, it is asking others to live as one wishes to live.

  It is not selfish to think for oneself. A man who does not think for himself does not think at all. It is grossly selfish to require of one's neighbor that he should think in the same way, and hold the same opinion.

CONVERSATION

᠍ Conversation is one of the loveliest of the arts.

᠍ Ultimately the bond of all companionship, whether in marriage or in friendship, is conversation.

᠍ Conversation should touch everything, but should concentrate itself on nothing.

᠍ The state of the weather is always an excusable exordium, but it is convenient to have a paradox or heresy on the subject always ready, so as to direct the conversation into other channels.

᠍ The art of conversation is really within the reach of almost everyone, except those who are morbidly truthful, or whose high moral worth requires to be sustained by a permanent gravity of demeanor, and a general dullness of mind.

᠍ Learned conversation is either the affectation of the ignorant or the profession of the mentally unemployed.

᠍ Recreation, not instruction, is the aim of conversation.

᠍ The maxim "If you find the company dull, blame yourself" seems to us somewhat optimistic.

᠍ One wants something that will encourage conversation, particularly at the end of the season when everyone has practically said whatever they had to say, which in most cases, was probably not much.

✍ Nobody, even in the provinces, should ever be allowed to ask an intelligent question about pure mathematics across a dinner table.

✍ In the case of meeting a genius and a duke at dinner, the good talker will try to raise himself to the level of the former and to bring the latter down to his own level. To succeed among one's social superiors one must have no hesitation in contradicting them.

✍ A man who can dominate a London dinner table can dominate the world.

✍ I adore them [London dinner parties]. The clever people never listen, and the stupid people never talk.

✍ One should never listen. To listen is a sign of indifference to one's hearers.

✍ It is a very dangerous thing to listen. If one listens one may be convinced; and a man who allows himself to be convinced by an argument is a thoroughly unreasonable person.

✍ It is only the intellectually lost who ever argue.

✍ I dislike arguments of any kind. They are always vulgar, and often convincing.

✍ Arguments are extremely vulgar, for everybody in good society holds exactly the same opinions.

CONVICTION

❧ The man who sees both sides of a question is a man who sees absolutely nothing at all.

❧ One should never take sides in anything. . . . Taking sides is the beginning of sincerity, and earnestness follows shortly afterwards, and the human being becomes a bore.

❧ To believe is very dull. To doubt is intensely engrossing. To be on the alert is to live, to be lulled into security is to die.

❧ I never approve, or disapprove, of anything now. It is an absurd attitude to take towards life. We are not sent into the world to air our moral prejudices.

❧ The things one feels absolutely certain about are never true. That is the fatality of Faith, and the lesson of Romance.

❧ A thing is not necessarily true because a man dies for it.

❧ No man dies for what he knows to be true. Men die for what they want to be true, for what some terror in their hearts tells them is not true.

CRIME AND PUNISHMENT

❧ Murder is always a mistake. One should never do anything that one cannot talk about after dinner.

❧ There is no essential incongruity between crime and culture. We cannot re-write the whole of history for the purpose of gratifying our moral sense of what should be.

⒢ Starvation, and not sin, is the parent of modern crime.

⒢ A community is infinitely more brutalized by the habitual employment of punishment, than it is by the occasional occurrence of crime.

⒢ As one reads history . . . one is absolutely sickened, not by the crimes that the wicked have committed, but by the punishments that the good have inflicted.

⒢ The more punishment is inflicted the more crime is produced.

⒢ The criminal classes are so close to us that even the policeman can see them. They are so far away from us that only the poet can understand them.

⒢ Crime belongs exclusively to the lower orders. . . . I should fancy that crime was to them what art is to us, simply a method of procuring extraordinary sensations.

⒢ To turn an interesting thief into a tedious honest man was not his [Jesus'] aim. He would have thought little of the Prisoners Aid Society and other modern movements of the kind.

⒢ Reformation is a much more painful process than punishment, is indeed punishment in its most aggravated and moral form—a fact which accounts for our entire failure as a community to reclaim that most interesting phenomenon who is called the confirmed criminal.

⒢ It is not the prisoners who need reformation. It is the prisons.

⒢ The only really humanizing influence in prison is the influence of the prisoners.

Prison life makes one see people and things as they really are. That is why it turns one to stone. It is the people outside who are deceived by the illusion of a life in constant motion.

To those who are in prison, tears are a part of every day's experience. A day in prison on which one does not weep is a day on which one's heart is hard, not a day on which one's heart is happy.

The most terrible thing about it [imprisonment] is not that it breaks one's heart—hearts are made to be broken—but that it turns one's heart to stone.

CRITICISM

Criticism is the highest form of autobiography.

There has never been a creative age that has not been critical also.

The highest Criticism, being the purest form of personal impression, is in its way more creative than creation.

The censure of the Puritan, whether real or affected, is always out of place in literary criticism, and shows a want of recognition of the essential distinction between art and life.

The moment criticism exercises any influence, it ceases to be criticism. The aim of the true critic is to try and chronicle his own moods, not to try to correct the masterpiece of others.

CRITICS

꧁ The critic has to educate the public; the artist has to educate the critic.

꧁ The true critic addresses not the artist ever but the public only.

꧁ The true critic is he who bears within himself the dreams and ideas and feelings of myriad generations, and to whom no form of thought is alien, no emotional impulse obscure.

꧁ The first duty of an art critic is to hold his tongue at all times, and upon all subjects.

꧁ Critics rarely know how to praise an artistic work. The fact is, it requires an artist to praise art; anyone can pick it to pieces.

꧁ It is exactly because a man cannot do a thing that he is the proper judge of it.

꧁ Technique is really personality. That is the reason why the artist cannot teach it, why the pupil cannot learn it, and why the aesthetic critic can understand it.

꧁ It is only by intensifying his own personality that the critic can interpret the personality of others, and the more strongly this personality enters into the interpretation, the more real the interpretation becomes, the more satisfying, the more convincing, and the more true.

꧁ A critic should be taught to criticize a work of art without making any reference to the personality of the author. This, in fact, is the beginning of criticism.

 ✍ The primary aim of the critic is to see the object as it really is not.

 ✍ I am always amused by the silly vanity of those writers and artists of our day who seem to imagine that the primary function of the critic is to chatter about their second-rate work.

 ✍ No publisher should ever express an opinion of the value of what he publishes. That is a matter entirely for the literary critic to decide. . . . A publisher is simply a useful middle-man. It is not for him to anticipate the verdict of criticism.

CRITIQUES

 ✍ The best play I ever slept through.

 ✍ It is a thoroughly well-intentioned book, and eminently suitable for invalids.

 ✍ As a general rule, his verse is full of pretty echoes of other writers, but in one sonnet he makes a distinct attempt to be original and the result is extremely depressing.

 ✍ *Astray: A Tale of a Country Town* is a very serious volume. It has taken four people to write it, and even to read it requires assistance.

 ✍ *Andiatoroctè* is the title of a volume of poems by the Rev. Clarence Walworth, of Albany, N.Y. It is a word borrowed from the Indians, and should, we think, be returned to them as soon as possible.

✍ Mr. Whistler . . . has found in [biographer] Mr. Walter Dowdeswell the most ardent of admirers, indeed, we might almost say the most sympathetic of secretaries.

✍ Mr. Whistler always spelt art, and we believe still spells it, with a capital "I."

✍ That he is indeed one of the very greatest masters of painting is my opinion. And I may add that in this opinion Mr. Whistler himself entirely concurs.

✍ As for borrowing Mr. Whistler's ideas about art, the only thoroughly original ideas I have ever heard him express have had reference to his own superiority as a painter over painters greater than himself.

✍ [George Meredith:] As a writer he has mastered everything, except language; as a novelist he can do everything except tell a story.

✍ Meredith is a prose Browning, and so is Browning.

✍ M. Zola . . . is determined to show that, if he has not got genius, he can at least be dull.

✍ [Guy de Maupassant:] He writes lurid little tragedies in which everybody is ridiculous; bitter comedies at which one cannot laugh for very tears.

✍ Mr. Henry James writes fiction as if it were a painful duty.

❧ [Rudyard Kipling:] He is our first authority on the second-rate, and has seen marvelous things through keyholes.

❧ Longfellow is a great poet only for those who never read poetry.

❧ Longfellow has no imitators, for of echoes themselves there are no echoes.

❧ In his very rejection of art Walt Whitman is an artist. . . . If Poetry has passed him by, Philosophy will take note of him.

DANGER

❧ To elope is cowardly. It's running away from danger. And danger has become so rare in modern life.

❧ Every profession in which a man is in constant danger of losing his life has something fine about it.

❧ How fond women are of doing dangerous things! It is one of the qualities in them that I admire most. A woman will flirt with anybody in the world as long as other people are looking on.

❧ An idea that is not dangerous is unworthy of being called an idea at all.

❧ Everything is dangerous. . . . If it wasn't so, life wouldn't be worth living.

❧ The one advantage of playing with fire . . . is that one never even gets singed. It is the people who don't know how to play with it who get burned up.

DEFINITIONS

☞ Scandal is gossip made tedious by morality.

☞ Tact . . . is an exquisite sense of the symmetry of things.

☞ Cynicism is merely the art of seeing things as they are instead of as they ought to be.

☞ What is a cynic? A man who knows the price of everything and the value of nothing.

☞ The sentimentalist is always a cynic at heart. Indeed sentimentality is merely the bank holiday of cynicism.

☞ A sentimentalist . . . is a man who sees an absurd value in everything, and doesn't know the market price of any single thing.

☞ A sentimentalist is simply a man who desires to have the luxury of an emotion without paying for it.

☞ Experience is the name everyone gives to their mistakes.

☞ Caricature is the tribute which mediocrity pays to genius.

☞ Indifference is the revenge the world takes on mediocrities.

☞ Democracy means simply the bludgeoning of the people by the people for the people.

☞ Drama is the meeting-place of art and life.

DESCRIPTIONS

☞ He is a typical Englishman, always dull and usually violent.

✺ A red-cheeked, white-whiskered creature who, like so many of his class, was under the impression that inordinate joviality can atone for an entire lack of ideas.

✺ He hasn't a single redeeming vice.

✺ He is old enough to know worse.

✺ Like all people who try to exhaust a subject, he exhausted his listeners.

✺ A man with a hideous smile and a hideous past. He is asked everywhere. No dinner party is complete without him.

✺ Many a woman has a past, but I am told that she has at least a dozen, and that they all fit.

✺ She wore far too much rouge last night and not quite enough clothes. That is always a sign of despair in a woman.

✺ She behaves as if she was beautiful. Most American women do. It is the secret of their charm.

✺ She was a curious woman, whose dresses always looked as if they had been designed in a rage and put on in a tempest.

✺ When she is in a very smart gown she looks like an *édition de luxe* of a bad French novel.

✺ She tried to look picturesque, but only succeeded in being untidy.

✺ An over-dressed woman of forty-seven, with a hooked nose, who was always trying to get herself compromised, but was so peculiarly plain that to her great disappointment no one would ever believe anything against her.

    ✑ She was usually in love with somebody, and, as her passion was never returned, she had kept all her illusions.

    ✑ She was one of those people who think that, if you say the same thing over and over a great many times, it becomes true in the end.

    ✑ [She] talks more and says less than anybody I ever met. She is made to be a public speaker.

    ✑ A dowdy dull girl, with one of those characteristic British faces, that, once seen, are never remembered.

DISSENT

    ✑ Discontent is the first step in the progress of a man or a nation.

    ✑ Disobedience, in the eyes of anyone who has read history, is man's original virtue. It is through disobedience that progress has been made, through disobedience and through rebellion.

    ✑ In art, as in politics, there is but one origin for all revolutions, a desire on the part of man for a nobler form of life, for a freer method and opportunity of expression.

    ✑ Agitators are a set of interfering, meddling people, who come down to some perfectly contented class of the community and sow the seeds of discontent amongst them. That is the reason why agitators are so absolutely necessary.

DREAMING AND ACTION

☞ It is the first duty of a gentleman to dream.

☞ A dreamer is one who can only find his way by moonlight, and his punishment is that he sees the dawn before the rest of the world.

☞ Society often forgives the criminal; it never forgives the dreamer.

☞ The one person who has more illusions than the dreamer is the man of action.

☞ It [action] is the last resource of those who know not how to dream.

☞ Action . . . becomes simply the refuge of people who have nothing whatsoever to do.

☞ We are never less free than when we try to act.

DUTY

☞ Duty is what one expects from others, it is not what one does oneself.

☞ Duty . . . merely means doing what other people want because they want it.

☞ My duty is a thing I never do, on principle.

☞ My duty to myself is to amuse myself terrifically.

☞ A sense of duty is like some horrible disease. It destroys the tissues of the mind, as certain complaints destroy the tissues of the body.

🙟 People are afraid of themselves nowadays. They have forgotten the highest of all duties, the duty that one owes to one's self.

🙟 The first duty in life is to be as artificial as possible. What the second duty is no one has as yet discovered.

🙟 A woman's first duty in life is to her dressmaker isn't it? What the second duty is no one has as yet discovered.

EDUCATION

🙟 Nothing that is worth knowing can be taught.

🙟 Fortunately, in England at any rate, education produces no effect whatsoever.

🙟 Just as the philanthropist is the nuisance of the ethical sphere, so the nuisance of the intellectual sphere is the man who is so occupied in trying to educate others that he has never had any time to educate himself.

🙟 Everybody who is incapable of learning has taken to teaching.

🙟 In examinations the foolish ask questions that the wise cannot answer.

🙟 Examinations are pure humbug from beginning to end. If a

man is a gentleman, he knows quite enough, and if he is not a gentleman, whatever he knows is bad for him.

❧ People never think of cultivating a young girl's imagination. It is the great defect of modern education.

❧ We teach people how to remember, we never teach them how to grow.

❧ In the summer term Oxford teaches the exquisite art of idleness, one of the most important things that any University can teach.

❧ Give children beauty, not the record of bloody slaughters and barbarous brawls as they call history, or of the latitudes and longitudes of places nobody cares to visit, as they call geography.

❧ Children have a natural antipathy to books—handicraft should be the basis of education.

❧ I would have a workshop attached to every school, and one hour a day given up to the teaching of simple decorative arts. It would be a golden hour to the children.

❧ A school should be the most beautiful place in every town and village—so beautiful that the punishment for undutiful children should be that they would be debarred from going to school the following day.

EMOTION

❧ Emotion for the sake of emotion is the aim of life.

❧ The secret of life is never to have an emotion that is unbe-

coming.

✍ There is always something ridiculous about the emotions of people whom one has ceased to love.

✍ It is only shallow people who require years to get rid of an emotion. A man who is master of himself can end a sorrow as easily as he can invent a pleasure.

✍ I cannot repeat an emotion. No one can, except sentimentalists.

✍ One of the facts of physiology is the desire of any very intensified emotion to be relieved of some emotion that is its opposite. Nature's example of dramatic effect is the laughter of hysteria or the tears of joy.

ENGLAND

✍ Beer, the Bible, and the seven deadly virtues have made our England what she is.

✍ We are in the native land of the hypocrite.

✍ In England, a man who can't talk morality twice a week to a large, popular, immoral audience is quite over as a serious politician. There would be nothing left for him as a profession except Botany or the Church.

✍ The English public always feels perfectly at its ease when a mediocrity is talking to it.

✍ [The English] have a miraculous power of turning wine into water.

✍ To disagree with three-fourths of the British public on all points is one of the first elements of sanity.

☞ The English public, as a mass, takes no interest in a work of art until it is told that the work in question is immoral.

☞ Of all people in the world the English have the least sense of the beauty of literature.

☞ One should not be too severe on English novels; they are the only relaxation of the intellectually unemployed.

☞ There are only two forms of writers in England, the unread and the unreadable.

☞ We have been able to have fine poetry in England because the public do not read it, and consequently they do not influence it.

☞ If the English had realized what a great poet he [Shelley] really was, they would have fallen on him with tooth and nail, and made his life as unbearable to him as they possibly could.

☞ England never appreciates a poet until he is dead.

☞ The English mind is always in a rage. The intellect of the race is wasted on the sordid and stupid quarrels of second-rate politicians or third-rate theologians.

☞ We were delighted and amused at the typical English way in which our ideas were misunderstood. They took our epigrams as earnest, and our parodies as prose.

FACTS

☞ If something cannot be done to check, or at least to modify, our monstrous worship of facts, Art will become sterile and beauty will pass away from the land.

☞ Facts are not merely finding a footing-place in history, but they are usurping the domain of Fancy and have invaded the kingdom of Romance. Their chilling touch is over everything. They are vulgarizing mankind.

☞ The English are always degrading truths into facts. When a truth becomes a fact it loses all intellectual value.

☞ It is hard to have a good story interrupted by a fact.

☞ The ancient historians gave us delightful fiction in the form of fact; the modern novelist presents us with dull facts under the guise of fiction.

☞ In the works of our own Carlyle, whose *French Revolution* is one of the most fascinating historical novels ever written, facts are either kept in their proper subordinate position, or else entirely excluded on the general grounds of dullness.

☞ In the wild struggle for existence, we want to have something that endures, so we fill our minds with rubbish and facts. . . . The mind of the thoroughly well-informed man is a dreadful thing. It is like bric-a-brac shop, all monsters and dust, with everything priced above its proper value.

FAMILY

☞ A family is a terrible encumbrance, especially when one is not married.

☞ Fathers should be neither seen nor heard. That is the only proper basis for family life.

❧ Families are so mixed nowadays. Indeed, as a rule, everybody turns out to be somebody else.

FASHION

❧ Fashion is merely a form of ugliness so unbearable that we are compelled to alter it every six months.

❧ Fashion is what one wears oneself. What is unfashionable is what other people wear.

❧ From the sixteenth century to our own day there is hardly any form of torture that has not been inflicted on girls, and endured by women, in obedience to the dictates of an unreasonable and monstrous Fashion.

❧ Whatever limits, constrains, and mutilates is essentially ugly, though the eyes of many are so blinded by custom that they do not notice the ugliness till it has become unfashionable.

❧ There are fashions in art just as there are fashions in dress, and perhaps none of us can quite free ourselves from the influence of custom and the influence of novelty.

FRIENDS AND ENEMIES

❧ An acquaintance that begins with a compliment is sure to develop into a real friendship. It starts in the right manner.

❧ Laughter is not at all a bad beginning for a friendship, and it is far the best ending for one.

✍ Friendship is far more tragic than love. It lasts longer.

✍ I always like to know everything about my new friends, and nothing about my old ones.

✍ It is a very dangerous thing to know one's friends.

✍ At the holy season of Easter one is supposed to forgive all one's friends.

✍ One has a right to judge a man by the effect he has over his friends.

✍ Formal courtesies will strain a close friendship.

✍ What is the good of friendship if one cannot say exactly what one means? Anybody can say charming things and try to please and to flatter, but a true friend always says unpleasant things, and does not mind giving pain.

✍ I choose my friends for their good looks, my acquaintances for their good characters, and my enemies for their good intellects. A man cannot be too careful in his choice of enemies. I have not got one who is a fool. They are all men of some intellectual power, and consequently they all appreciate me.

✍ Be careful to choose your enemies well. Friends don't much matter. But the choice of enemies is very important.

✍ Next to having a staunch friend is the pleasure of having a brilliant enemy.

✍ I would sooner lose my best friend than my worst enemy. To have friends, you know, one need only be good-natured; but when a man has no enemy left there must be something mean about him.

    ▪ Every effect that one produces gives one an enemy. To be popular one must be a mediocrity.

GENERATIONS

    ▪ Children begin by loving their parents. After a time they judge them. Rarely, if ever, do they forgive them.

    ▪ Few parents nowadays pay any regard to what their children say to them. The old-fashioned respect for the young is fast dying out.

    ▪ There are so many sons who won't have anything to do with their fathers, and so many fathers who won't speak to their sons.

    ▪ There is always something about an heir to a crown unwholesome to his father.

    ▪ The longer I live. . . , the more keenly I feel that whatever was good enough for our fathers is not good enough for us.

    ▪ It is enough that our fathers have believed. They have exhausted the faith-faculty of the species. Their legacy to us is the skepticism of which they were afraid.

    ▪ No age borrows the slang of its predecessor.

GEOGRAPHY

    ▪ The two most remarkable bits of scenery in the States are undoubtedly Delmonico's and the Yosemite Valley.

ᴓ Chicago is a sort of monster-shop, full of bustle and bores. Political life at Washington is like political life in a suburban vestry. Baltimore is amusing for a week, but Philadelphia is dreadfully provincial; and though one can dine in New York, one could not dwell there.

ᴓ It is an odd thing, but everyone who disappears is said to be seen in San Francisco. It must be a delightful city, and possess all the attractions of the next world.

ᴓ San Francisco has the most lovely surroundings of any city except Naples.

ᴓ California is an Italy without its art.

ᴓ In no place is society more free and cordial and ready to give a friendly reception to a stranger than in California. In no part of the world is the individual more free from restraint.

ᴓ When I look at the map and see what an awfully ugly-looking country Australia is, I feel as if I want to go there to see if it cannot be changed into a more beautiful form.

ᴓ This gray, monstrous London of ours, with its myriads of people, its sordid sinners, and its splendid sins.

ᴓ London is too full of fogs . . . and serious people. . . . Whether the fogs produce the serious people or whether the serious people produce the fogs, I don't know.

ᴓ While in London one hides everything, in Paris one reveals everything.

ℝ The great superiority of France over England is that in France every bourgeois wants to be an artist, whereas in England every artist wants to be a bourgeois.

ℝ We Irish are too poetical to be poets; we are a nation of brilliant failures, but we are the greatest talkers since the Greeks.

ℝ If one could only teach the English how to talk, and the Irish how to listen, society here would be quite civilized.

ℝ I don't like Switzerland: it has produced nothing but theologians and waiters.

ℝ A map of the world that does not include Utopia is not worth even glancing at, for it leaves out the one country at which Humanity is always landing. And when Humanity lands there, it looks out, and, seeing a better country, sets sail. Progress is the realization of Utopias.

GOVERNMENT

ℝ In an evil moment the Philanthropist made his appearance, and brought with him the mischievous idea of Government.

ℝ All modes of government are failures.

ℝ Life under a good government is rarely dramatic; life under a bad government is always so.

ℝ Now that the House of Commons is trying to become useful, it does a great deal of harm.

ℝ Only people who look dull ever get into the House of Commons, and only people who are dull ever succeed there.

↜ There is this to be said in favor of the despot, that he, being an individual, may have culture, while the mob, being a monster, has none.

↜ There are three kinds of despots. There is the despot who tyrannizes over the body. There is the despot who tyrannizes over the soul. There is the despot who tyrannizes over the soul and body alike. The first is called the Prince. The second is called the Pope. The third is called the People.

↜ Those who try to lead the people can only do so by following the mob. It is through the voice crying in the wilderness that the ways of the gods must be prepared.

↜ One who is an Emperor and King may stoop down to pick up a brush for a painter, but when the democracy stoops down it is merely to throw mud.

↜ It is indeed a burning shame that there should be one law for men and another law for women. I think that there should be no law for anybody.

↜ *I like no law at all;*
Were there no law there'd be no law-breakers,
So all men would be virtuous.

↜ To be entirely free, and at the same time entirely dominated by law, is the eternal paradox of human life that we realize at every moment.

↜ All authority is quite degrading. It degrades those who exercise it, and degrades those over whom it is exercised.

🔗 Wherever there is a man who exercises authority there is a man who resists authority.

HISTORY

🔗 History is merely gossip.

🔗 The details of history . . . are always wearisome and usually inaccurate.

🔗 History never repeats itself. The historians repeat each other.

🔗 Anybody can make history. Only a great man can write it.

🔗 The one duty we owe to history is to re-write it.

🔗 We cannot re-write the whole of history for the purpose of gratifying our moral sense of what should be.

🔗 To give an accurate description of what has never occurred is not merely the proper occupation of the historian, but the inalienable privilege of any man of parts and culture.

HUMAN NATURE

🔗 The more one analyzes people, the more all reasons for analysis disappear. Sooner or later one comes to that dreadful universal thing called human nature.

🔗 The only thing that one really knows about human nature is that it changes.

🔗 The systems that fail are those that rely on the permanency of human nature, and not on its growth and development. The error of Louis XIV was that he thought human nature would always be the same. The result of his error was the French Revolution.

 ⚭ I will predict, accurately, all human behavior except that which governs the human heart.

 ⚭ The real fool, such as the gods mock or mar, is he who does not know himself.

 ⚭ To know anything about oneself one must know all about others.

 ⚭ The great things of life leave one unmoved. . . . We regret the burden of their memory, and have anodynes against them. But the little things, the things of the moment, remain with us.

 ⚭ Find expression for a sorrow, and it will become dear to you. Find expression for a joy, and you intensify its ecstasy.

 ⚭ Every little action of the common day makes or unmakes character . . . what one has done in the secret chamber one has some day to cry aloud on the housetops.

 ⚭ The only thing that ever consoles man for the stupid things he does is the praise he always gives himself for doing them.

 ⚭ There is a luxury in self-reproach. When we blame ourselves we feel that no one else has a right to blame us. It is the confession, not the priest, that gives us absolution.

 ⚭ Humanity will always love Rousseau for having confessed his sins, not to a priest, but to the world.

❧ The reason we all like to think so well of others is that we are all afraid for ourselves. The basis of optimism is sheer terror.

❧ We think that we are generous because we credit our neighbor with the possession of those virtues that are likely to be a benefit to us. We praise the banker that we may overdraw our account, and find good qualities in the highwayman in the hope that he may spare our pockets.

❧ It is what we fear that happens to us.

❧ Great antipathy shows secret affinity.

❧ Whenever there is hatred between two people there is bond or brotherhood of some kind.

❧ It is in the brain, and the brain only, that the great sins of the world take place.

❧ Each man sees his own sin in Dorian Gray. What Dorian Gray's sins are no one knows. He who finds them has brought them.

❧ *We are each our own devil, and we make*
   This world our hell.

❧ Each of us has Heaven and Hell in him.

HUMOR

❧ Even in acts of charity there should be some sense of humor.

❧ Humanity takes itself too seriously. It is the world's original sin. If the cavemen had known how to laugh, History would have been different.

  🖙 Laughter is the primeval attitude towards life—a mode of approach that survives only in artists and criminals.

  🖙 Where one laughs there is no immorality; immorality and seriousness begin together.

  🖙 The world has always laughed at its own tragedies, that being the only way in which it has been able to bear them. . . . Consequently, whatever the world has treated seriously belongs to the comedy side of things.

  🖙 You can produce tragic effects by introducing comedy. A laugh in an audience does not destroy terror, but, by relieving it, aids it. Never be afraid that by raising a laugh you destroy tragedy. On the contrary, you intensify it.

INTELLECT

  🖙 To expect the unexpected shows a thoroughly modern intellect.

  🖙 Intellect . . . destroys the harmony of any face. The moment one sits down to think, one becomes all nose, or all forehead, or something horrid. Look at the successful men in any of the learned professions. How perfectly hideous they are! Except, of course, in the Church. But then in the Church they don't think. A bishop keeps on saying at the age of eighty what he was told to say when he was eighteen, and as a natural consequence he always looks delightful.

꘎ Thinking is the most unhealthy thing in the world, and people die of it just as they die of any other disease.

꘎ All thought is immoral. Its very essence is destruction. If you think of anything, you kill it. Nothing survives being thought of.

꘎ Thought is wonderful, but adventure is more wonderful still.

꘎ While, in the opinion of society, Contemplation is the gravest thing of which any citizen can be guilty, in the opinion of the highest culture it is the proper occupation of man.

꘎ To do nothing at all is the most difficult thing in the world, the most difficult and the most intellectual.

JOURNALISM

꘎ Bad manners make a journalist.

꘎ Modern journalists . . . always apologize to one in private for what they have written against one in public.

꘎ There is much to be said in favor of modern journalism. By giving us the opinions of the uneducated, it keeps us in touch with the ignorance of the community.

꘎ Journalists record only what happens. What does it matter what happens? It is only the abiding things that are interesting, not the horrid incidents of everyday life.

꘎ The journalist is always reminding the public of the existence of the artist. That is unnecessary of him. He is always reminding the artist of the existence of the public. That is indecent of him.

‍‍‍ In centuries before ours the public nailed the ears of journalists to the pump. That was quite hideous. In this country journalists have nailed their own ears to the keyhole. That is much worse.

‍‍‍ Spies are of no use nowadays. . . . The newspapers do their work instead.

‍‍‍ The conscience of an editor is purely decorative.

‍‍‍ In the old days men had the rack. Now they have the Press.

LIFE

‍‍‍ Life is terribly deficient in form. Its catastrophes happen in the wrong way and to the wrong people. There is a grotesque horror about its comedies, and its tragedies seem to culminate in farce.

‍‍‍ Life is much too important a thing ever to talk seriously about.

‍‍‍ Life is never fair.

‍‍‍ Life goes faster than Realism, but Romanticism is always in front of Life.

‍‍‍ Life itself is an art, and has its modes of style no less than the arts that seek to express it.

‍‍‍ The aim of life is self-development. To realize one's nature perfectly—that is what each of us is here for.

❧ To live is the rarest thing in the world. Most people exist, that is all.

❧ There are few things easier than to live badly and to die well.

❧ One should live as if there were not death.

❧ One can live for years sometimes without living at all, and then all life comes crowding into one single hour.

❧ We can have in life but one great experience at best, and the secret of life is to reproduce that experience as often as possible.

❧ Don't tell me that you have exhausted Life. When a man says that one knows that life has exhausted him.

❧ To become the spectator of one's own life is to escape the suffering of life.

❧ Life cheats us with shadows. We ask it for pleasure. It gives it to us, with bitterness and disappointment in its train.

❧ What a pity in life that we only get our lessons when they are of no use to us!

❧ *For he who lives more lives than one*
More deaths than one must die.

LITERATURE

❧ Literature always anticipates life. It does not copy it, but molds it to its purpose. The nineteenth century, as we know it, is largely an invention of Balzac.

🖙 There is no modern literature outside France.

🖙 French prose, even in the hands of the most ordinary writers, is always readable, but English prose is detestable.

🖙 Anybody can write a three-volume novel. It merely requires a complete ignorance of both life and literature.

🖙 Many a young man starts in life with a natural gift for exaggeration which, if nurtured in congenial and sympathetic surroundings, or by the imitation of the best models, might grow into something really great and wonderful. But, as a rule, he comes to nothing. He either falls into careless habits of accuracy, or takes to frequenting the society of the aged and well-informed. . . . In a short time he develops a morbid and unhealthy faculty of truth-telling, begins to verify all statements made in his presence, has no hesitation in contradicting people who are much younger than himself, and often ends by writing novels which are so life-like that no one can possibly believe in their probability.

🖙 I hate vulgar realism in literature. The man who could call a spade a spade should be compelled to use one.

🖙 Are there not books that can make us live more in one single hour than life can make us live in a score of shameful years?

🖙 It was said of Trollope that he increased the number of our acquaintances without adding to our visiting list; but after reading the *Comédie Humaine* [by Balzac] one begins to believe that the only real people are the people who have never existed.

🖙 A steady course of Balzac reduces our living friends to shadows, and our acquaintances to the shadows of shades. . . . It is pleasanter to have the entrée to Balzac's society than to receive cards from all the duchesses in Mayfair.

  ❧ The only form of fiction in which real characters do not seem out of place is history.

  ❧ To introduce real people into a novel or a play is a sign of an unimaginative mind, a coarse, untutored observation, and an entire absence of style.

  ❧ If a novelist is base enough to go to life for his personages he should at least pretend that they are creations, and not boast of them as copies.

  ❧ There is a great deal to be said in favor of reading a novel backwards. The last page is, as a rule, the most interesting and when one begins with the catastrophe or the *dénouement* one feels on pleasant terms of equality with the author.

  ❧ To know the vintage and quality of a wine one need not drink the whole cask. It must be perfectly easy in half an hour to say whether a book is worth anything or worth reading. Ten minutes are really sufficient, if one has the instinct for form. Who wants to wade through a dull volume? One tastes it, and that is quite enough.

  ❧ If one cannot enjoy reading a book over and over again, there is no use reading it at all.

  ❧ There is no such thing as a moral or an immoral book. Books are well-written, or badly written.

✍ The books that the world calls immoral books are books that show the world its own shame.

✍ The fact of a man being a poisoner is nothing against his prose.

✍ The Celtic element in literature is extremely valuable, but there is absolutely no excuse for shrieking "Shillelagh!" and "O'Gorrah!"

✍ There is no such thing as Shakespeare's Hamlet. If Hamlet has something of the definiteness of a work of art, he has also all the obscurity that belongs to life. There are as many Hamlets as there are melancholies.

✍ Schopenhauer has analyzed the pessimism that characterizes modern thought, but Hamlet invented it.

✍ No one survives being over-estimated, nor is there any surer way of destroying an author's reputation than to glorify him without judgment and to praise him without tact.

✍ There is always something peculiarly impotent about the violence of a literary man. It seems to bear no reference to facts, for it is never kept in check by action. It is simply a question of adjectives and rhetoric, of exaggeration and over-emphasis.

LOVE

✍ All love is a tragedy.

✍ Misunderstanding . . . is the basis of love.

❧ Love is not fashionable anymore, the poets have killed it.

❧ True love suffers, and is silent.

❧ To be in love is to surpass oneself.

❧ I cannot live without the atmosphere of Love: I must love and be loved, whatever price I pay for it.

❧ Love does not traffic in a marketplace, nor use a huckster's scales. Its joy, like the joy of the intellect, is to feel itself alive. The aim of Love is to love.

❧ Love makes people good.

❧ Love can canonize people. The saints are those who have been most loved.

❧ Love is the sacrament of life.

❧ Love is merely passion with a holy name.

❧ Everyone is worthy of love, except he who thinks he is.

❧ It is not the perfect, but the imperfect, who have need of love. It is when we are wounded by our own hands, or by the hands of others, that love should come to cure us—else what use is love at all?

❧ Love can heal all wounds.

❧ It is love, and not German philosophy, that is the true explanation of this world, whatever may be the explanation of the next.

❧ Each time that one loves is the only time one has ever

loved. Difference of object does not alter singleness of passion. It merely intensifies it.

🙠 Those who are faithful know only the trivial side of love: it is the faithless who know love's tragedies.

🙠 Faithfulness is to the emotional life what consistency is to the life of the intellect—simply a confession of failure.

🙠 What a fuss people make about fidelity! Why, even in love it is purely a question for physiology. It has nothing to do with our own will.

🙠 Lust . . . makes one love all that one loathes.

🙠 It is difficult not to be unjust to what one loves.

🙠 *Yet each man kills the thing he loves,*
   By each let this be heard
   Some do with a bitter look,
   Some with a flattering word,
   The coward does it with a kiss,
   The brave man with a sword!

🙠 One should always be in love. That is the reason one should never marry.

MARRIAGE

🙠 The proper basis for marriage is a mutual misunderstanding.

🙠 Married life is merely a habit, a bad habit.

The real drawback to marriage is that it makes one unselfish. And unselfish people are colorless. They lack individuality.

How marriage ruins a man! It's as demoralizing as cigarettes, and far more expensive.

The happiness of a married man . . . depends on the people he has not married.

Every experience is of value, and, whatever one may say against marriage, it is certainly an experience.

The one charm of marriage is that it makes a life of deception absolutely necessary for both parties.

The world has grown so suspicious of anything that looks like a happy married life.

Marriage is hardly a thing that one can do now and then . . . except in America.

The American freedom of divorce . . . has at least the merit of bringing into marriage a new element of romantic uncertainty. . . . Where the bond can be easily broken, its very fragility makes its strength, and reminds the husband that he should always try to please, and the wife that she should never cease to be charming.

Divorces are made in heaven.

It's most dangerous nowadays for a husband to pay attention to his wife in public. It always makes people think he beats her when they are alone.

Nowadays everybody is jealous of everyone else, except, of course, husband and wife.

Twenty years of romance make a woman look like a ruin; but twenty years of marriage make her something like a public building.

Girls never marry the men they flirt with. Girls don't think it right.

Men marry because they are tired; women because they are curious. Both are disappointed.

When a woman marries again it is because she detested her first husband. When a man marries again, it is because he adored his first wife. Women try their luck; men risk theirs.

MEN AND WOMEN

Men know life too early. . . . Women know life too late. That is the difference between men and women.

Women are never disarmed by compliments. Men always are. That is the difference between the sexes.

The soul of woman is beauty, as the soul of man is strength. If the two could be combined in the one being we should have the perfection sought by art since art began.

Women love us for our defects. If we have enough of them they will forgive us everything, even our intellects.

They [women] always want one to be good. And if we are

good when they meet us, they don't love us at all. They like to find us quite irretrievably bad, and to leave us quite unattractively good.

 The only way a woman can ever reform a man is by boring him so completely that he loses all possible interest in life.

 Women are not meant to judge us, but to forgive us when we need forgiveness. Pardon, not punishment, is their mission.

 When a man does exactly what a woman expects him to do she doesn't think much of him. One should always do what a woman doesn't expect, just as one should always say what she doesn't understand. The result is invariably perfect sympathy on both sides.

 Talk to every woman as if you loved her, and to every man as if he bored you, and at the end of your first season you will have the reputation of possessing the most perfect social tact.

 When a man has once loved a woman, he will do anything for her, except continue to love her.

 A man can be happy with any woman, as long as he does not love her.

 Men always want to be a woman's first love. That is their clumsy vanity. . . . Women have a more subtle instinct about things. What [they] like is to be a man's last romance.

 There is only one real tragedy in a woman's life. The fact that the past is always her lover, and her future invariably her husband.

Men when they woo us call us pretty children,
  Tell us we have not wit to make our lives.
  And so they mar them for us. Did I say woo?
  We are their chattels, and their common slaves,
  Less dear than the poor hound that licks their hand,
  Less fondled than the hawk upon their wrist.
  Woo, did I say? bought rather, sold and bartered.

Between men and women there is no friendship possible. There is passion, enmity, worship, love, but no friendship.

Wicked women bother one. Good women bore one. That is the only difference between them.

The amount of women in London who flirt with their own husbands is perfectly scandalous. It looks so bad. It is simply washing one's clean linen in public.

Every woman is a rebel, and usually in wild revolt against herself.

If you want to know what a woman really means—which, by the way, is always a dangerous thing to do—look at her, don't listen to her.

Women have a wonderful instinct about things. They can discover everything except the obvious.

No woman should ever be quite accurate about her age. It looks so calculating.

One should never trust a woman who tells one her real age. A woman who would tell one that, would tell one anything.

✒ It is only very ugly or very beautiful women who ever hide their faces.

✒ Crying is the refuge of plain women but the ruin of pretty ones.

✒ The one charm of the past is that it is the past. But women never know when the curtain has fallen. They always want a sixth act, and as soon as the interest in the play is entirely over, they propose to continue it.

✒ Women defend themselves by attacking, just as they attack by sudden and strange surrenders.

✒ If a woman wants to hold a man she has merely to appeal to what is worst in him.

✒ There's nothing in the world like the devotion of a married woman. It's a thing no married man knows anything about.

✒ Perplexity and mistrust fan affection into passion, and so bring about those beautiful tragedies that alone make life worth living. Women once felt this, while men did not, and so women once ruled the world.

✒ No man has any real success in this world unless he has got women to back him, and women rule society. If you have not got women on your side, you are quite over. You might just as well be a barrister, or a stockbroker, or a journalist at once.

MISCELLANY

✒ It is always nice to be expected, and not to arrive.

✍ Three addresses always inspire confidence, even in tradesmen.

✍ The man who possesses a permanent address, and whose name is to be found in the Directory, is necessarily limited and localized. Only the tramp has absolute liberty of living.

✍ A man whose desire is to be something separate from himself, to be a Member of Parliament, or a successful grocer, or a prominent solicitor, or a judge, or something equally tedious, invariably succeeds in being what he wants to be. That is his punishment.

✍ Each of the professions means a prejudice.

✍ Even the disciple has his uses. He stands behind one's throne, and at the moment of one's triumph whispers in one's ear that, after all, one is immortal.

✍ Every great man nowadays has his disciples, and it is always Judas who writes the biography.

✍ Everyone should keep someone else's diary.

✍ I never travel without my diary. One should always have something sensational to read in the train.

✍ I only care to see doctors when I am in perfect health; then they comfort one, but when one is ill they are most depressing.

✍ One can survive everything nowadays, except death, and live down anything except a good reputation.

✍ We are all in the gutter, but some of us are looking at the stars.

✐ Between the famous and the infamous there is but one step, if so much as one.

✐ Knaves nowadays do look so honest that honest folk are forced to look like knaves so as to be different.

✐ Formerly we used to canonize our great men; nowadays we vulgarize them.

✐ To make a good salad is to be a brilliant diplomatist—the problem is entirely the same in both cases. To know exactly how much oil one must put with one's vinegar.

✐ Nothing looks so like innocence as an indiscretion.

✐ There are many things that we would throw away if we were not afraid that others might pick them up.

✐ There is always something infinitely mean about other people's tragedies.

✐ The real tragedies of life occur in such an inartistic manner that they hurt us by their crude violence, their absolute incoherence, their absurd want of meaning, their entire lack of style.

✐ Why is it that one runs to one's ruin? Why has destruction such a fascination?

MISFORTUNE

✐ Misfortunes one can endure—they come from outside, they are accidents. But to suffer for one's own faults—ah !—there is the sting of life.

One needs misfortunes to live happily.

To live in happiness, you must know some unhappiness in life.

The happy people of the world have their value, but only the negative value of foils. They throw up and emphasize the beauty and the fascination of the unhappy.

What seem to us bitter trials are often blessings in disguise.

What fire does not destroy, it hardens.

Suffering is a terrible fire; it either purifies or destroys.

Suffering and the community of suffering makes people kind.

The secret of life is suffering.

While to propose to be a better man is a piece of unscientific cant, to have become a *deeper* man is the privilege of those who have suffered.

There is no truth comparable to Sorrow. There are times when Sorrow seems to me to be the only truth.

Sorrow, being the supreme emotion of which man is capable, is at once the type and test of all great Art.

Behind Joy and Laughter there may be a temperament, coarse, hard, and callous. But behind Sorrow there is always Sorrow. Pain, unlike pleasure, wears no mask.

MODERATION

Moderation is a fatal thing. Enough is as bad as a meal. More than enough is as good as a feast.

๛ Nothing is good in moderation. You cannot know the good in anything till you have torn the heart out of it by excess.

๛ All excess, as well as all renunciation, brings its own punishment.

๛ Nothing succeeds like excess.

MODERNITY

๛ Pure modernity of form is always somewhat vulgarizing.

๛ Modernity of form and modernity of subject matter are entirely and absolutely wrong.

๛ To be modern is the only thing worth being nowadays.

๛ Nothing is so dangerous as being too modern; one is apt to grow old-fashioned quite suddenly.

๛ It is only the modern that ever becomes old-fashioned.

MODERN LIFE

๛ In modern life nothing produces such an effect as a good platitude. It makes the whole world kin.

๛ We are born in an age when only the dull are treated seriously.

๛ We live in an age of the over-worked, and the under-educated; the age in which people are so industrious that they become absolutely stupid.

✍ We live in an age that reads too much to be wise, and that thinks too much to be beautiful.

✍ People should not mistake the means of civilization for the end. The steam engine and the telephone depend entirely for their value on the use to which they are put.

✍ The value of the telephone is the value of what two people have to say.

✍ The type-writing machine, when played with expression, is not more annoying than the piano when played by a sister or near relation.

✍ They [automobiles], like all machines, are more willful than animals—nervous, irritable, strange things.

✍ The train that whirls an ordinary Englishman through Italy at the rate of forty miles an hour and finally sends him home without any memory of that lovely country but that he was cheated by a courier at Rome, or that he got a bad dinner at Verona, does not do him or civilization much good.

✍ Of what use is it to a man to travel sixty miles an hour? . . . Is he any better for it? Why, a fool can buy a railway ticket and travel sixty miles an hour. Is he any less a fool?

✍ Why does not science, instead of troubling itself about sunspots, which nobody ever saw, or, if they did, ought not to speak about; why does not science busy itself with drainage and sanitary engineering? Why does it not clean the streets and free the rivers from pollution?

MOODS

✒ Only one thing remains infinitely fascinating to me, the mystery of moods. To be master of these moods is exquisite, to be mastered by them more exquisite still.

✒ You people who go in for being consistent have just as many moods as others have. The only difference is that your moods are rather meaningless.

✒ There must be no mood with which one cannot sympathize, no dead mode of life that one cannot make alive.

✒ To yield to all one's moods is to really live.

MORALITY

✒ Morality is simply the attitude we adopt towards people whom we personally dislike.

✒ There is no such thing as morality, for there is no general rule of spiritual health; it is all personal, individual.

✒ There is no such thing as a good influence. . . . All influence is immoral—immoral from the scientific point of view.

✒ Neither art nor science knows anything of moral approval or disapproval.

✒ Science is out of the reach of morals, for her eyes are fixed upon eternal truths. Art is out of the reach of morals, for her eyes are fixed upon things beautiful and immortal and ever-changing. To morals belong the lower and less intellectual spheres.

✍ Any preoccupation with ideas of what is right or wrong in conduct shows an arrested intellectual development.

✍ Modern morality consists in accepting the standard of one's age. I consider that for any man of culture to accept the standard of his age is a form of the grossest immorality.

✍ A high moral tone can hardly be said to conduce very much to either one's health or one's happiness.

✍ Manners are of more importance than morals.

✍ The moral is too obvious.

✍ I never came across anyone in whom the moral sense was dominant who was not heartless, cruel, vindictive, log-stupid, and entirely lacking in the smallest sense of humanity. Moral people, as they are termed, are simple beasts.

✍ In old days . . . to be a bit better than one's neighbor was considered excessively vulgar and middle-class. Nowadays, with our modern mania for morality, everyone has to pose as a paragon of purity, incorruptibility, and all the other seven deadly virtues.

✍ [Al]though of all poses a moral pose is the most offensive, still to have a pose at all is something.

MUSIC

✍ Music is the art . . . which most completely realizes the artistic idea, and is the condition to which all the other arts are constantly aspiring.

✎ *A quality*
 Which music sometimes has, being the Art
 Which is most nigh to tears and memory.

✎ Music . . . creates for one a past of which one has been ignorant, and fills one with a sense of sorrows that have been hidden from one's tears.

✎ If one plays good music, people don't listen, and if one plays bad music, people don't talk.

✎ If one hears bad music, it is one's duty to drown it in conversation.

✎ I like Wagner's music better than anybody's. It is so loud that one can talk the whole time without people hearing what one says.

✎ Musical people are so absurdly unreasonable. They always want one to be perfectly dumb at the very moment when one is longing to be absolutely deaf.

NATURE

✎ The things of nature do not really belong to us; we should leave them to our children as we have received them.

✎ In nature there is, for me at any rate, healing power.

✎ We all look at Nature too much, and live with her too little.

✎ If Nature had been comfortable, mankind would never have invented architecture.

✍ Nature, which makes nothing durable, always repeats itself so that nothing which it makes may be lost.

✍ Nature is no great mother who has borne us. She is our creation. It is in our brain that she quickens to life.

✍ Nature is always behind the age.

✍ Nature is elbowing her way into the charmed circle of art.

✍ A thing in Nature becomes much lovelier if it reminds us of a thing in Art, but a thing in Art gains no real beauty through reminding us of a thing in Nature.

✍ The more we study Art, the less we care for Nature. What Art really reveals to us is Nature's lack of design, her curious crudities, her extraordinary monotony, her absolutely unfinished condition. Nature has good intentions, of course, but, as Aristotle once said, she cannot carry them out.

✍ Art is our spirited protest, our gallant attempt to teach Nature her proper place.

✍ One touch of Nature may make the whole world kin, but two touches of Nature will destroy any work of Art.

✍ Whenever we have returned to Life and Nature, our work has always become vulgar, common, and uninteresting.

✍ I hate views—they are only made for bad painters.

✍ When I look at a landscape, I cannot help seeing all its defects.

It is not necessary to have great natural wonders at home to develop art. The landscapes of Italy are all-satisfying, and so the Italian artist does not reproduce them. You must go to the cloudy, the misty lands, for great landscape painters.

Nobody of any real culture . . . ever talks nowadays about the beauty of the sunset. Sunsets are quite old-fashioned. They belong to a time when Turner was the last note in art. To admire them is a distinct sign of provincialism of temperament.

At twilight nature becomes a wonderfully suggestive effect, and is not without loveliness, though perhaps its chief use is to illustrate quotations from the poets.

PEOPLE

Only dull people are brilliant at breakfast.

There are only two kinds of people who are really fascinating—people who know absolutely everything, and people who know absolutely nothing.

All charming people, I fancy, are spoiled. It is the secret of their attraction.

I never take any notice of what common people say, and I never interfere with what charming people do.

PERSONALITY

Personality is a very mysterious thing. A man cannot always be estimated by what he does. He may keep the law, and yet be worthless. He may break the law, and yet be fine. He may be bad without ever doing anything bad. He may commit a sin against society, and yet realize through that sin his true perfection.

ℐ One must accept a personality as it is. One must never regret that a poet is drunk, but that drunkards are not always poets.

ℐ One regrets the loss even of one's worst habits. Perhaps one regrets them the most. They are such an essential part of one's personality.

ℐ Nothing is so fatal to a personality as the keeping of promises, unless it be telling the truth.

PLAGIARISM

ℐ Accusations of plagiarism . . . proceed either from the thin colorless lips of impotence, or from the grotesque mouths of those who, possessing nothing of their own, fancy that they can gain a reputation for wealth by crying out that they have been robbed.

ℐ I can hardly imagine that the public are in the very smallest degree interested in the shrill shrieks of "Plagiarism" that proceed from time to time out of the lips of silly vanity or incompetent mediocrity.

ℐ Of course I plagiarize. It is the privilege of the appreciative man.

ℐ Never say you have "adapted" anything from anyone. Appropriate what is already yours—for to publish anything is to make it public property.

✍ It is only the unimaginative who ever invent. The true artist is known by the use he makes of what he annexes, and he annexes everything.

✍ True originality is to be found rather in the use made of a model than in the rejection of all models . . . we should not quarrel with the reed if it whispers to us the music of the lyre.

PLAYS

✍ The actable value of a play has nothing whatsoever to do with its value as a work of art. . . . It is . . . not by the mimes that the muses are to be judged.

✍ Every word in a play has a musical as well as an intellectual value, and must be made expressive of a certain emotion.

✍ The tears that we shed at a play are a type of the exquisite sterile emotions that it is the function of Art to awaken. We weep, but we are not wounded. We grieve, but our grief is not bitter.

✍ No spectator of art needs a more perfect mood of receptivity than the spectator of a play. The moment he seeks to exercise authority he becomes the avowed enemy of Art, and of himself.

✍ I don't believe there is a single dramatic critic in London who would deliberately set himself to misrepresent the work of any dramatist—unless, of course, he personally disliked the dramatist, or had some play of his own he wished to produce at the same theater, or had an old friend among the actors.

✍ I never write plays for anyone. I write plays to amuse myself. After, if people want to act in them, I sometimes allow them to do so.

✍ There are two ways of disliking my plays. One is to dislike them, the other is to like *Earnest.*

✍ I am not nervous on the night that I am producing a new play. I am exquisitely indifferent. My nervousness ends at the last dress rehearsal. I know then what effect my play, as presented upon the stage, has produced upon me. My interest in the play ends there, and I feel curiously envious of the public—they have such wonderfully fresh emotions in store for them.

PLEASURE

✍ Pleasure is the only thing one should live for.

✍ Pleasure is Nature's test, her sign of approval. When man is happy he is in harmony with himself and his environment.

✍ No civilized man ever regrets a pleasure, and no uncivilized man ever knows what a pleasure is.

✍ What consoles one nowadays is not repentance but pleasure.

✍ I adore simple pleasures. They are the last refuge of the complex.

✍ A cigarette is the perfect type of a perfect pleasure. It is exquisite, and it leaves one unsatisfied. What more can one want?

☞ Better to take pleasure in a rose than to put its root under a microscope.

☞ I don't regret for a single moment having lived for pleasure. I did it to the full, as one should do everything that one does to the full. There was no pleasure I did not experience.

☞ Not happiness! Above all, not happiness. Pleasure!

POETRY

☞ Poetry is for our highest moods, when we wish to be with the gods.

☞ Poetry should be like a crystal; it should make life more beautiful and less real.

☞ Poetry may be said to need far more self-restraint than prose. Its conditions are more exquisite. It produces its effects by more subtle means.

☞ Lying and poetry are arts—arts, as Plato saw, not unconnected with each other.

☞ There seems to be some curious connection between piety and poor rhymes.

☞ All bad poetry springs from genuine feeling. To be natural is to be obvious, and to be obvious is to be inartistic.

☞ Every century that produces poetry is, so far, an artificial century, and the work that seems to us the most natural and simple product of its time is probably the result of the most deliberate and self-conscious effort.

  There are two ways of disliking poetry, one way is to dislike it, the other is to read Pope.

  Most people become bankrupt through having invested too heavily in the prose of life. To have ruined oneself over poetry is an honor.

  Books of poetry by young writers are usually promissory notes that are never met.

POETS

  When man acts he is a puppet. When he describes he is a poet.

  Poets are always ahead of science; all the great discoveries of science have been stated before in poetry.

  A poet without hysterics is rare.

  Little poets are an extremely interesting study. The best of them have often some new beauty to show us, and though the worst of them may bore yet they rarely brutalize.

  A great poet, a really great poet, is the most unpoetical of creatures. But inferior poets are absolutely fascinating. The worse their rhymes are, the more picturesque they look. The mere fact of having published a book of second-rate sonnets makes a man quite irresistible. He lives the poetry that he cannot write. The others write the poetry that they dare not realize.

  [Poets] know how useful passion is for publication. Nowadays a broken heart will run to many editions.

  A poet can survive everything but a misprint.

PRINCIPLES

❧ I like persons better than principles, and I like persons with no principles better than anything else in the world.

❧ I don't like principles. . . . I prefer prejudices.

❧ It is personalities, not principles, that move the age.

THE PUBLIC

❧ The public have an insatiable curiosity to know everything, except what is worth knowing.

❧ The public is wonderfully tolerant. It forgives everything except genius.

❧ The public is largely influenced by the *look* of a book. So are we all. It is the only artistic thing about the public.

❧ Public Opinion . . . is an attempt to organize the ignorance of the community.

❧ Public opinion exists only where there are no ideas.

❧ I am very fond of the public, and, personally, I always patronize the public very much.

QUIPS

❧ He never touches water: it goes to his head at once.

❧ He knew the precise psychological moment when to say nothing.

🖎 There are a hundred things I want not to say to you.

🖎 Whenever people agree with me, I always feel I must be wrong.

🖎 My own business always bores me to death. I prefer other people's.

🖎 Nowadays we are all of us so hard up, that the only pleasant things to pay are compliments.

🖎 To partake of two luncheons in one day would not be liberty. It would be license.

🖎 When I am in trouble, eating is the only thing that consoles me. Indeed, when I am in really great trouble . . . I refuse everything except food and drink.

🖎 Why don't you ask me how I am? I like people to ask me how I am. It shows a wide-spread interest in my health.

🖎 I seem to have heard that observation before. . . . It has all the vitality of error and all the tediousness of an old friend.

🖎 The simplicity of your character makes you exquisitely incomprehensible to me.

🖎 I am a little too old now, myself, to trouble about setting a good example, but I always admire people who do.

🖎 I don't at all like knowing what people say of me behind my back. It makes me far too conceited.

🖎 On the staircase stood several Royal Academicians, disguised as artists.

℞ Varnishing is the only process with which the Royal Academicians are thoroughly familiar.

℞ I remember a clergyman who wanted to be a lunatic, or a lunatic who wanted to be a clergyman, I forget which, but I know the Court of Chancery investigated the matter, and decided he was quite sane.

℞ She ultimately was so broken-hearted that she went into a convent, or on to the operatic stage, I forget which. No; I think it was decorative art-needlework she took up.

℞ She tried to found a *salon,* and only succeeded in opening a restaurant.

REASON

℞ I can stand brute force, but brute reason is quite unbearable. There is something unfair about its use. It is hitting below the intellect.

℞ Science can never grapple with the irrational. That is why it has no future before it.

℞ I wonder who it was defined man as a rational animal. It was the most premature definition ever given. Man is many things, but he is not rational.

℞ One is tempted to define man as a rational animal who always loses his temper when he is called upon to act in accordance with the dictates of reason.

✍ The fatal errors of life are not due to man's being unreasonable: an unreasonable moment may be one's finest moment. They are due to man's being logical. There is a wide difference.

✍ It is not logic that makes men reasonable, nor the science of ethics that makes men good.

RELATIVES

✍ Relations are simply a tedious pack of people, who haven't got the remotest knowledge of how to live, nor the smallest instinct about when to die.

✍ Relations never lend one any money, and won't give one credit, even for genius. They are a sort of aggravated form of the public.

✍ I can't help detesting my relations. I suppose it comes from the fact that none of us can stand other people having the same faults as ourselves.

✍ After a good dinner one can forgive anybody, even one's own relations.

✍ I have never heard any man mention his brother. The subject seems distasteful to most men.

ROMANCE

✍ When one is in love one always begins by deceiving oneself and one always ends by deceiving others. That is what the world calls a romance.

   ✐ The worst of having a romance is that it leaves one so unromantic.

   ✐ There is no such thing as a romantic experience; there are romantic memories, and there is the desire for romance—that is all. Our most fiery moments of ecstasy are merely shadows of what somewhere else we have felt, or of what we long some day to feel.

   ✐ It is very romantic to be in love, but there is nothing romantic about a definite proposal. Why, one may be accepted. One usually is, I believe. Then the excitement is all over.

   ✐ The very essence of romance is uncertainty. If I ever get married, I'll certainly try to forget the fact.

   ✐ Lovers are happiest when they are in doubt.

   ✐ The romance of life is that one can love so many people and marry but one.

   ✐ Women . . . spoil every romance by trying to make it last forever.

   ✐ Every romance that one has in one's life is a romance lost to one's art.

   ✐ How silly to write on pink paper! It looks like the beginning of a middle-class romance.

   ✐ Romance is the privilege of the rich, not the profession of the unemployed.

SCANDAL

✍ The basis for every scandal is an immoral certainty.

✍ One should never make one's *début* with a scandal. One should reserve that to give an interest to one's old age.

✍ I love scandals about other people, but scandals about myself don't interest me. They have not got the charm of novelty.

✍ Scandals used to lend charm, or at least interest, to a man— now they crush him.

SIN

✍ What is termed Sin is an essential element of progress. Without it the world would stagnate or grow old, or become colorless.

✍ Sin is the only real color-element left in modern life.

✍ By its curiosity Sin increases the experience of the race. . . . In its rejection of the current notions about morality it is one with the higher ethics.

✍ Sins of the flesh are nothing. They are maladies for physicians to cure, if they should be cured. Sins of the soul alone are shameful.

✍ The body sins once, and has done with its sin, for action is a mode of purification. Nothing remains then but the recollection of a pleasure, or the luxury of a regret.

Ɂ There were sins whose fascination was more in the memory than in the doing of them; strange triumphs that gratified the pride more than the passions, and gave to the intellect a quickened sense of joy.

Ɂ The only horrible thing in the world is *ennui*.... That is the one sin for which there is no forgiveness.

Ɂ There is no sin except stupidity.

Ɂ *Oh, can it be*
There is some immortality in sin,
Which virtue has not?

Ɂ *They do not sin at all*
Who sin for love.

Ɂ The sick do not ask if the hand that smooths their pillow is pure, nor the dying care if the lips that touch their brow have known the kiss of sin.

Ɂ Nothing makes one so vain as being told that one is a sinner.

Ɂ The only difference between the saint and the sinner is that every saint has a past, and every sinner has a future.

SINCERITY

Ɂ A little sincerity is a dangerous thing, and a great deal of it is absolutely fatal.

ⓒ We are dominated by the fanatic, whose worst vice is his sincerity.

ⓒ What people call insincerity is simply a method by which we can multiply our personalities.

SOCIETY

ⓒ The canons of good society are, or should be, the same as the canons of art. Form is absolutely essential to it.

ⓒ Society, civilized society at least, is never ready to believe anything to the detriment of those who are both rich and fascinating. It feels instinctively that manners are of more importance than morals, and, in its opinion, the highest respectability is of much less value than the possession of a good *chef.*

ⓒ Society is wonderfully delightful. To be in it is merely a bore. But to be out of it is simply a tragedy.

ⓒ Never speak disrespectfully of society. . . . Only people who can't get into it do that.

ⓒ To get into the best society, nowadays, one has either to feed people, amuse people, or shock people.

ⓒ [London society] is entirely composed now of beautiful idiots and brilliant lunatics. Just what Society should be.

ⓒ Other people are quite dreadful. The only possible society is oneself.

SOUL

❧ Those who see any difference between soul and body have neither.

❧ When one comes in contact with the soul it makes one simple as a child, as Christ said one should be.

❧ The soul itself, the soul of each one of us, is to each one of us a mystery. It hides in the dark and broods, and consciousness cannot tell us of its workings.

❧ To recognize that the soul of a man is unknowable is the ultimate achievement of Wisdom. The final mystery is oneself. When one has weighed the sun in a balance, and measured the steps of the moon, and mapped out the seven heavens star by star, there still remains oneself. Who can calculate the orbit of his own soul?

❧ Behind the perfection of a man's style, must lie the passion of a man's soul.

STYLE

❧ One's style is one's signature always.

❧ The best style is that which seems an unconscious result rather than a conscious aim.

❧ Style largely depends on the way the chin is worn.

❧ Sentiment is all very well for the buttonhole. But the essential thing for a necktie is style. A well-tied tie is the first serious step in life.

ᐧᐧᐧ In the mode of the knotting of one's necktie or the conduct of one's cane there is an entire creed of life.

ᐧᐧᐧ In matters of grave importance, style, not sincerity, is the vital thing.

SUCCESS

ᐧᐧᐧ Success is a science; if you have the conditions, you get the result.

ᐧᐧᐧ There is something about success, actual success, that is a little unscrupulous, something about ambition that is unscrupulous always.

ᐧᐧᐧ There is something vulgar in all success. The greatest men fail—or seem to the world to have failed.

ᐧᐧᐧ Anybody can sympathize with the sufferings of a friend, but it requires a very fine nature—it requires, in fact, the nature of a true Individualist—to sympathize with a friend's success.

SUICIDE

ᐧᐧᐧ Suicide is the greatest compliment that one can pay to society.

ᐧᐧᐧ Sometimes I think that the artistic life is a long and lovely suicide, and am not sorry that it is so.

SYMPATHY

ᐧᐧᐧ Humanitarian Sympathy wars against Nature, by securing the survival of the failure.

🖙 The real harm that emotional sympathy does is that it limits knowledge, and so prevents us from solving any single social problem.

🖙 While sympathy with joy intensifies the sum of joy in the world, sympathy with pain does not really diminish the amount of pain. It may make man better able to endure evil, but the evil remains.

🖙 It is much more easy to have sympathy with suffering than it is to have sympathy with thought.

🖙 All sympathy is fine, but sympathy with suffering is the least fine mode. It is tainted with egotism. It is apt to become morbid. There is in it a certain element of terror for our own safety.

TALK

🖙 Language is the noblest instrument we have, either for the revealing or the concealing of thought; talk itself is a sort of spiritualized action.

🖙 Actions are the first tragedy in life, words are the second. Words are perhaps the worst. Words are merciless.

🖙 There is no mode of action, no form of emotion, that we do not share with the lower animals. It is only by language that we rise above them, or above each other—by language, which is the parent, and not the child of thought.

Lots of people act well . . . but very few people talk well, which shows that talking is much more the difficult thing of the two, and much the finer thing also.

It is very much more difficult to talk about a thing than to do it.

I love talking about nothing. . . . It is the only thing I know anything about.

Whenever people talk to me about the weather, I always feel certain that they mean something else.

It is much cleverer to talk nonsense than to listen to it . . . , and a much rarer thing too, in spite of all the public may say.

The only possible form of exercise is to talk, not to walk.

TEMPTATION

I can resist everything except temptation.

The only way to get rid of a temptation is to yield to it. Resist it, and your soul grows sick with longing for the things it has forbidden to itself.

There are terrible temptations that it requires strength, strength and courage, to yield to. To stake all one's life on one throw—whether the stakes be power or pleasure, I care not—there is no weakness in that. There is a horrible, a terrible courage.

Life's aim, if it has one, is simply to be always looking for temptations. There are not nearly enough. I sometimes pass a whole day without coming across a single one.

THEOLOGY

❧ The history of theology is the history of madness.

❧ Ordinary theology has long since converted its gold into lead, and words and phrases that once touched the heart of the world have become wearisome and meaningless through repetition.

❧ To die for one's theological beliefs is the worst use a man can make of his life.

❧ Martyrdom was to me merely a tragic form of skepticism, an attempt to realize by fire what one had failed to do by faith.

❧ Skepticism is the beginning of Faith.

❧ In a Temple everyone should be serious, except the thing that is worshiped.

❧ Imaginative people will invariably be religious people for the simple reason that religion has sprung from the imagination.

❧ When I think about Religion at all, I feel as if I would like to found an order for those who cannot believe.

❧ Everything to be true must become a religion. And agnosticism should have its ritual no less than faith. It has sown its martyrs, it should reap its saints, and praise God daily for having hidden Himself from man.

꧁ Religions die when they are proved to be true. Science is the record of dead religions.

꧁ In matters of religion, it [truth] is simply the opinion that has survived.

꧁ Religion consoles some. Its mysteries have all the charm of a flirtation, a woman once told me.

꧁ When I think of all the harm that book [the Bible] has done, I despair of ever writing anything equal to it.

꧁ The terror of society, which is the basis of morals, the terror of God, which is the secret of religion—these are the two things that govern us.

꧁ The Catholic Church is for saints and sinners alone. For respectable people the Anglican Church will do.

꧁ Catholicism is the only religion to die in.

꧁ When the gods wish to punish us they answer our prayers.

꧁ Prayer must never be answered: if it is, it ceases to be prayer and becomes correspondence.

꧁ I think half-an-hour's warping of the inner man daily is greatly conducive to holiness.

꧁ Missionaries are the divinely provided food for destitute and underfed cannibals. Whenever they are on the brink of starvation, Heaven, in its infinite mercy, sends them a nice plump missionary.

When you convert someone else to your own faith, you cease to believe in it yourself.

It is so easy to convert others. It is so difficult to convert oneself.

He who would lead a Christlike life is he who is perfectly and absolutely himself.

How else but through a broken heart
May Lord Christ enter in?

Where there is Sorrow there is holy ground.

TIME

Time is waste of money.

When one pays a visit it is for the purpose of wasting other people's time, not one's own.

He was always late on principle, his principle being that punctuality is the thief of time.

I am not punctual myself, I know, but I do like punctuality in others.

No one should make unpunctuality a formal rule, and degrade it to a virtue.

TOWN AND COUNTRY

Town life nourishes and perfects all the more civilized elements in man—Shakespeare wrote nothing but doggerel lampoon before he came to London and never penned a line after he left.

✍ One can only write in cities.

✍ When one is in town one amuses oneself. When one is in the country one amuses other people. It is excessively boring.

✍ Anybody can be good in the country. There are no temptations there.

✍ It is pure, unadulterated country life. They get up early because they have so much to do, and go to bed early because they have so little to think about.

✍ I don't think any one at all morally responsible for what he or she does at an English country house.

TRIVIA

✍ The trivial in thought and action is charming.

✍ We should treat all trivial things of life very seriously, and all the serious things of life with sincere and studied triviality.

✍ People are never so trivial as when they take themselves very seriously.

TRUTH AND LIES

✍ Truth is entirely and absolutely a matter of style.

✍ The truth is rarely pure and never simple.

⁓ The truth is a thing I get rid of as soon as possible.

⁓ To know the truth one must imagine myriads of falsehoods.

⁓ The way of paradoxes is the way of truth. To test Reality we must see it on the tight rope. When the Verities become acrobats we can judge them.

⁓ If truth has her revenge upon those who do not follow her, she is often pitiless to her worshipers.

⁓ A truth ceases to be true when more than one person believes in it.

⁓ It is a terrible thing for a man to find out suddenly that all his life he has been speaking nothing but the truth.

⁓ If one tells the truth, one is sure, sooner or later, to be found out.

⁓ To lie finely is an art, to tell the truth is to act according to nature.

⁓ The only form of lying that is absolutely beyond reproach is lying for its own sake.

⁓ The aim of the liar is simply to charm, to delight, to give pleasure. He is the very basis of civilized society.

⁓ Society sooner or later must return to its lost leader, the cultured and fascinating liar.

⁓ If a man is sufficiently unimaginative to produce evidence in support of a lie, he might just as well speak the truth at once.

UNDERSTANDING

☙ What one really wants is not to be either blamed or praised, but to be understood.

☙ The praise of the man who can't understand me is quite as injurious as the abuse of any enemy can be.

☙ It is only mediocrities and old maids who consider it a grievance to be misunderstood.

☙ I live in terror of not being misunderstood.

☙ He is fond of being misunderstood. It gives him a post of vantage.

☙ Incomprehensibility is a gift. Not everyone has it.

☙ Only the great masters of style ever succeed in being obscure.

☙ Nowadays to be intelligible is to be found out.

VANITY

☙ It is curious how vanity helps the successful man and wrecks the failure.

☙ To love oneself is the beginning of a lifelong romance.

☙ Egotism is not without its attractions. When people talk to us about others they are usually dull. When they talk to us about themselves they are nearly always interesting.

To be an Egoist, one must have an Ego. It is not everyone who says "I, I" who can enter into the Kingdom of Art.

Humility is for the hypocrite, modesty for the incompetent.

Conceit is the privilege of the creative.

Conceit is one of the greatest of the virtues, yet how few people recognize it as a thing to aim at and to strive after. In conceit many a man and woman has found salvation, yet the average person goes on all fours groveling after modesty.

The only thing that sustains one through life is the consciousness of the immense inferiority of everybody else.

It would be unfair to expect other people to be as remarkable as oneself.

VIEWS

Nothing is so aggravating as calmness.

Nothing pains me except stupidity.

The ugly and the stupid have the best of it in this world. They can sit at their ease and gape at the play. If they know nothing of victory, they are at least spared the knowledge of defeat.

Industry is the root of all ugliness.

Dullness is the coming of age of seriousness.

Questions are never indiscreet. Answers sometimes are.

The word "natural" means all that is middle class, all that is of the essence of Jingoism, all that is colorless and without form and void. It might be a beautiful word, but it is the most debased coin in the currency of language.

The word "practical" is nearly always the last refuge of the uncivilized.

Civilization is not by any means an easy thing to attain to. There are only two ways by which man can reach it. One is by being cultured, the other by being corrupt.

Psychology is in its infancy as a science. I hope, in the interests of art, it will always remain so.

For he to whom the present is the only thing that is present, knows nothing of the age in which he lives.

One could never pay too high a price for any sensation.

To have a capacity for a passion and not to realize it is to make oneself incomplete and limited.

I don't believe in progress: but I do believe in the stagnation of human perversity.

I have the greatest contempt for optimism.

It is always a silly thing to give advice, but to give good advice is absolutely fatal.

I always pass on good advice. It is the only thing to do with it. It is never any use to oneself.

❧ Never buy a thing you don't want merely because it is dear.

❧ Whenever one has anything unpleasant to say, one should always be quite candid.

❧ People who count their chickens before they are hatched act very wisely: because chickens run about so absurdly that it is almost impossible to count them accurately.

❧ Create yourself. Be yourself your poem.

❧ One should absorb the color of life, but one should never remember its details. Details are always vulgar.

❧ Details are the only things that interest.

❧ It is only about things that do not interest one that one can give a really unbiased opinion, which is no doubt the reason why an unbiased opinion is always absolutely valueless.

❧ It is only in voluntary associations that man is fine.

❧ One can always be kind to people about whom one cares nothing. That is why English family life is so pleasant.

❧ It is a very unimaginative nature that only cares for people on their pedestals.

❧ The only things worth doing are those that the world is surprised at.

❧ Nothing is worth doing except what the world says is impossible.

❧ Man can believe the impossible, but man can never believe the improbable.

One should always be a little improbable.

Secrecy seems to be the one thing that can make modern life mysterious or marvelous to us. The commonest thing is delightful if one only hides it.

Most men and women are forced to perform parts for which they have no qualifications. Our Guildensterns play Hamlet for us, and our Hamlets have to jest like Prince Hal. The world is a stage, but the play is badly cast.

An eternal smile is much more wearisome than a perpetual frown. The one sweeps away all possibilities, the other suggests a thousand.

Ambition is the last refuge of the failure.

Consistency is the last refuge of the unimaginative.

We are never more true to ourselves than when we are inconsistent.

It is often said that force is no argument. That, however, entirely depends on what one wants to prove.

One should always play fairly . . . when one has the winning cards.

Good resolutions are useless attempts to interfere with scientific laws. Their origin is pure vanity. Their result is absolutely nil. They give us, now and then, some of those luxurious sterile emotions that have a certain charm for the weak. . . . They are simply checks that men draw on a bank where they have no account.

⟋ There is only one thing in the world worse than being talked about, and that is not being talked about.

⟋ In this world there are only two tragedies. One is not getting what one wants, and the other is getting it.

⟋ The well-bred contradict other people. The wise contradict themselves.

⟋ There is no such thing as an omen. Destiny does not send us heralds. She is too wise or too cruel for that.

⟋ Everyone is born a king, and most people die in exile, like most kings.

⟋ If a man needs an elaborate tombstone in order to remain in the memory of his country, it is clear that his living at all was an act of absolute superfluity.

VIRTUE

⟋ I would sooner have fifty unnatural vices than one unnatural virtue.

⟋ Don't be led astray into the paths of virtue.

⟋ You can't make people good by Act of Parliament.

⟋ If you want to mar a nature, you have merely to reform it.

⟋ It is a sign of a noble nature to refuse to be broken by force. Never attempt to reform a man. Men never repent.

& It is absurd to divide people into good and bad. People are either charming or tedious.

& What are called good women may have terrible things in them, mad moods of recklessness, assertion, jealousy, sin. Bad women, as they are termed, may have in them sorrow, repentance, pity, sacrifice.

& If one intends to be good one must take it up as a profession. It is quite the most engrossing one in the world.

& Nowadays so many conceited people go about Society pretending to be good, that I think it shows rather a sweet and modest disposition to pretend to be bad.

& If you pretend to be good the world takes you very seriously. If you pretend to be bad, it doesn't. Such is the astounding stupidity of optimism.

& Leading a double life, pretending to be wicked and being really good all the time . . . would be hypocrisy.

& To be good, according to the vulgar standard of goodness, is obviously quite easy. It merely requires a certain amount of sordid terror, a certain lack of imaginative thought, and a certain low passion for middle-class respectability.

& To be good is to be in harmony with oneself. Discord is to be forced to be in harmony with others.

& One is not always happy when one is good; but one is always good when one is happy.

The best way to make children good is to make them happy.

Wickedness is a myth invented by good people to account for the curious attractiveness of others.

Good people do a great deal of harm in the world. Certainly the greatest harm they do is that they make badness of such extraordinary importance.

One is punished for the good as well as the evil that one does.

If we lived long enough to see the results of our actions it may be that those who call themselves good would be filled with a dull remorse and those whom the world calls evil stirred by a noble joy.

It is a very poor consolation to be told that the man who has given one a bad dinner, or poor wine, is irreproachable in his private life.

VULGARITY

Vulgarity is simply the conduct of other people.

All crime is vulgar, just as all vulgarity is crime.

As long as war is regarded as wicked, it will always have its fascination. When it is looked upon as vulgar, it will cease to be popular.

It is very vulgar to talk like a dentist when one isn't a dentist. It produces a false impression.

WEALTH

✍ What this century worships is wealth. The God of this century is wealth.

✍ Young people, nowadays, imagine that money is everything . . . and when they grow older they know it.

✍ Private property has really harmed Individualism, and obscured it, by confusing a man with what he possesses.

✍ The true perfection of man lies, not in what man has, but in what man is.

✍ When one has learnt, however inadequately, what a lovely thing gratitude is, one's feet go lightly over sand or sea, and one finds a strange joy revealed to one, the joy of counting up, not what one possesses, but what one owes.

✍ God used poverty often as a means of bringing people to Him, and used riches never, or but rarely.

WORK

✍ Work is the curse of the drinking classes.

✍ Man is made for something better than disturbing dirt. All work of that kind should be done by a machine.

✍ Hard work is simply the refuge of people who have nothing whatever to do.

✍ Cultivated idleness seems to me to be the proper occupation for man.

WRITING

Idleness gives one the mood in which to write, isolation the conditions.

Romantic surroundings are the worst surroundings possible for a romantic writer.

The difficulty under which the novelists of our day labor seems to me to be this: if they do not go into society, their books are unreadable; and if they do go into society, they have no time left for writing.

Writing to newspapers has a deteriorating influence on style. People get violent, and abusive, and lose all sense of proportion, when they enter that curious journalistic arena in which the race is always to the noisiest.

Even prophets correct their proofs.

To learn how to write English prose I have studied the prose of France.

I write because it gives me the greatest possible artistic pleasure to write. If my work pleases the few I am gratified. As for the mob, I have no desire to be a popular novelist. It is far too easy.

I don't write to please cliques. I write to please myself.

I wrote when I did not know life; now that I do know the meaning of life, I have no more to write. Life cannot be written; life can only be lived.

Byplay

VERA, OR THE NIHILISTS

MICHAEL: It is not so romantic a thing to lose one's head, Prince Paul.

PRINCE PAUL: No, but it must often be very dull to keep it. Don't you find that sometimes?

———

PRINCE PAUL: . . . I find these Cabinet Councils extremely tiring.

PRINCE PETROVICH: Naturally, you are always speaking.

PRINCE PAUL: No; I think it must be that I have to listen sometimes. It is so exhausting not to talk.

THE DUCHESS OF PADUA

DUKE OF PADUA: Come hither, fellow! What is your name?

CITIZEN: Dominick, sir.

DUKE: A good name! Why were you called Dominick?

CITIZEN: Marry, because I was born on Saint George's day.

DUKE: A good reason! Here is a ducat for you!
Will you not cry for me God save the Duke?
CITIZEN: God save the Duke.
DUKE: Nay! Louder, fellow, louder.
CITIZEN: God save the Duke!
DUKE: More lustily, fellow, put more heart in it!
Here is another ducat for you.
CITIZEN: God save the Duke!
DUKE: Why, gentlemen, this simple fellow's love
Touches me much.

———

MAFFIO: It is most strange when women love their lords,
And when they love them not it is most strange.
JEPPO: What a philosopher thou art, Petrucci!
MAFFIO: Ay! I can bear the ills of other men,
Which is philosophy.

LADY WINDERMERE'S FAN

LADY WINDERMERE: Believe me, you are better than most other men, and I sometimes think you pretend to be worse.

LORD DARLINGTON: We all have our little vanities, Lady Windermere.

———

DUCHESS OF BERWICK: I won't let you know my daughter, you are far too wicked.

LORD DARLINGTON: Don't say that, Duchess. As a wicked man, I am a complete failure. Why, there are lots of people who say I have never really done anything wrong on the whole course of my life. Of course they only say it behind my back.

———

DUMBY: What a mystery you are!

LADY PLYMDALE: I wish *you* were!

DUMBY: I am—to myself. I am the only person in the world I should like to know thoroughly; but I don't see any chance of it just at present.

———

LORD AUGUSTUS: It is a great thing to come across a woman who thoroughly understands one.

DUMBY: It is an awfully dangerous thing. They always end by marrying one.

———

LORD AUGUSTUS: Mrs. Erlynne has a future before her.

DUMBY: Mrs. Erlynne has a past before her.

LORD AUGUSTUS: I prefer a woman with a past. They're always so demmed amusing to talk to.

CECIL GRAHAM: Well, you'll have lots of topics of conversation with her, Tuppy.

———

DUMBY: How long could you love a woman who didn't love you, Cecil?

CECIL GRAHAM: A woman who didn't love me? Oh, all my life!

DUMBY: So could I. But it's so difficult to meet one.

A WOMAN OF NO IMPORTANCE

LADY CAROLINE: I don't think that England should be represented abroad by an unmarried man, Jane. It might lead to complications.

LADY HUNSTANTON: You are too nervous, Caroline. Believe me, you are too nervous. Besides, Lord Illingworth may marry one day. I was in hopes he would have married Lady Kelso. But I believe he said her family was too large. Or was it her feet? I forget which. I regret it very much. She was made to be an ambassador's wife.

LADY CAROLINE: She certainly has a wonderful faculty of remembering people's names, and forgetting their faces.

———

LADY STUTFIELD: Ah! The world was made for men and not for women.

MRS. ALLONBY: Oh, don't say that, Lady Stutfield. We have a much better time than they have. There are far more things forbidden to us than are forbidden to them.

———

LADY STUTFIELD: The world says that Lord Illingworth is very, very wicked.

LORD ILLINGWORTH: But what world says that, Lady Stutfield? It must be the next world. This world and I are on excellent terms.

LADY STUTFIELD: Every one *I* know says you are very, very wicked.

LORD ILLINGWORTH: It is perfectly monstrous the way people go about, nowadays, saying things against one behind one's back that are absolutely and entirely true.

———

KELVIL: I am afraid you don't appreciate America, Lord Illingworth. It is a very remarkable country, especially considering its youth.

LORD ILLINGWORTH: The youth of America is their oldest tradition. It has been going on now for three hundred years. To hear them talk we would imagine they were in their first childhood. As far as civilization goes they are in their second.

———

MRS. ALLONBY: Horrid word "health."

LORD ILLINGWORTH: Silliest word in our language, and one knows so well the popular idea of health. The English country gentleman galloping after a fox—the unspeakable in full pursuit of the uneatable.

KELVIL: May I ask, Lord Illingworth, if you regard the House of Lords as a better institution than the House of Commons?

LORD ILLINGWORTH: A much better institution of course. We in the House of Lords are never in touch with public opinion. That makes us a civilized body.

———

LADY CAROLINE: You believe good of every one, Jane. It is a great fault.

LADY STUTFIELD: Do you really, really think, Lady Caroline, that one should believe evil of every one?

LADY CAROLINE: I think it is much safer to do so, Lady Stutfield. Until, of course, people are found out to be good. But that requires a great deal of investigation nowadays.

———

LORD ILLINGWORTH: . . . Nothing spoils a romance so much as a sense of humor in the woman.

MRS. ALLONBY: Or the want of it in the man.

———

LORD ILLINGWORTH: What do you call a bad man?

MRS. ALLONBY: The sort of man who admires innocence.

LORD ILLINGWORTH: And a bad woman?

MRS. ALLONBY: Oh! the sort of woman a man never gets tired of.

———

LORD ILLINGWORTH: I never intend to grow old. The soul is born old but grows young. That is the comedy of life.

MRS. ALLONBY: And the body is born young and grows old. That is life's tragedy.

————

MRS. ALLONBY: You should certainly know Ernest, Lady Stutfield. It is only fair to tell you beforehand he has got no conversation at all.

LADY STUTFIELD: I adore silent men.

MRS. ALLONBY: Oh, Ernest isn't silent. He talks the whole time. But he has got no conversation.

————

LADY CAROLINE: Oh, women have become so highly educated, Jane, that nothing should surprise us nowadays, except happy marriages. They apparently are getting very rare.

MRS. ALLONBY: Oh, they're quite out of date.

LADY STUTFIELD: Except amongst the middle classes, I have been told.

MRS. ALLONBY: How like the middle classes!

————

MRS. ALLONBY: More marriages are ruined nowadays by the common sense of the husband than by anything else. How can a woman be expected to be happy with a man who insists on treating her as if she was a perfectly rational being?

LADY HUNSTANTON: My dear!

MRS. ALLONBY: Man, poor, awkward, reliable, necessary man belongs to a sex that has been rational for millions and millions of years. He can't help himself. It is in his race. The History of Woman is very different. We have always been picturesque protests against the mere existence of common sense. We saw its dangers from the first.

————

LADY CAROLINE: There are a great many things you haven't got in America, I am told, Miss Worsley. They say you have no ruins, and no curiosities.

MRS. ALLONBY: What nonsense! They have their mothers and their manners.

———

LADY HUNSTANTON: Most women in London, nowadays, seem to furnish their rooms with nothing but orchids, foreigners, and French novels. But here we have the room of a sweet saint. Fresh natural flowers, books that don't shock one, pictures that one can look at without blushing.

MRS. ALLONBY: But I like blushing.

LADY HUNTINGTON: Well, there is a good deal to be said for blushing, if one can do it at the proper moment. Poor dear Hunstanton used to tell me I didn't blush nearly often enough. But then he was so very particular. He wouldn't let me know any of his men friends, except those who were over seventy, like poor Lord Ashton; who afterwards, by the way, was brought into the Divorce Court. A most unfortunate case.

MRS. ALLONBY: I delight in men over seventy. They always offer one the devotion of a lifetime. I think seventy an ideal age for a man.

———

LORD ILLINGWORTH: We men know life too early.

MRS. ARBUTHNOT: And we women know life too late. That is the difference between men and women.

AN IDEAL HUSBAND

SIR ROBERT CHILTERN: May I ask, at heart, are you an optimist or a pessimist? Those seem to be the only two fashionable religions left to us nowadays.

MRS. CHEVELEY: Oh, I'm neither. Optimism begins in a broad grin, and Pessimism ends with blue spectacles. Besides, they are both of them merely poses.

SIR ROBERT CHILTERN: You prefer to be natural?

MRS. CHEVELEY: Sometimes. But it is such a very difficult pose to keep up.

———

MABEL CHILTERN: You are always telling me of your bad qualities, Lord Goring.

LORD GORING: I have only told you half of them as yet, Miss Mabel!

MABEL CHILTERN: Are the others very bad?

LORD GORING: Quite dreadful! When I think of them at night I go to sleep at once.

———

LORD GORING: Extraordinary thing about the lower classes in England—they are always losing their relations.

PHIPPS: Yes, my lord! They are extremely fortunate in that respect.

———

LORD GORING: I am glad you have called. I am going to give you some good advice.

MRS. CHEVELEY: Oh! pray don't. One should never give a woman anything that she can't wear in the evening.

———

LADY MARKBY: . . . In my time, of course, we were taught not to understand anything. That was the old system, and wonderfully interesting it was. I assure you that the amount of things I and my poor sister were taught not to understand was quite extraordinary. But modern women understand everything, I am told.

MRS. CHEVELEY: Except their husbands. That is the one thing the modern woman never understands.

LADY MARKBY: And a very good thing too, dear, I dare say. It might break up many a happy home if they did.

———

LORD CAVERSHAM: You seem to me to be living entirely for pleasure.

LORD GORING: What else is there to live for, father? Nothing ages like happiness.

THE IMPORTANCE OF BEING EARNEST

ALGERNON: You don't seem to realize, that in married life three is company and two is none.

JACK: That, my dear young friend, is the theory that the corrupt French Drama has been propounding for the last fifty years.

ALGERNON: Yes; and that the happy English home has proved in half the time.

———

LADY BRACKNELL: Good-afternoon, dear Algernon, I hope you are behaving very well.

ALGERNON: I'm feeling very well, Aunt Augusta.

LADY BRACKNELL: That's not quite the same thing. In fact the two things rarely go together.

———

LADY BRACKNELL: . . . I had some crumpets with Lady Harbury, who seems to me to be living entirely for pleasure now.

ALGERNON: I hear her hair has turned quite gold from grief.

———

LADY BRACKNELL: . . . Do you smoke?

JACK: Well, yes, I must admit I smoke.

LADY BRACKNELL: I am glad to hear it. A man should always have an occupation of some kind. There are far too many idle men in London as it is.

———

LADY BRACKNELL: . . . Are your parents living?

JACK: I have lost both my parents.

LADY BRACKNELL: Both? . . . To lose one parent, Mr. Worthing, may be regarded as a misfortune; to lose both looks like carelessness.

———

ALGERNON: All women become like their mothers. That is their tragedy. No man does. That's his.

JACK: Is that clever?

ALGERNON: It is perfectly phrased! And quite as true as any observation in civilized life should be.

———

JACK: I am sick to death of cleverness. Everybody is clever nowadays. You can't go anywhere without meeting clever people. The thing has become an absolute public nuisance. I wish to goodness we had a few fools left.

ALGERNON: We have.

JACK: I should extremely like to meet them. What do they talk about?

ALGERNON: The fools? Oh! about the clever people of course.

JACK: What fools.

ALGERNON: I hope to-morrow will be a fine day, Lane.

LANE: It never is, sir.

ALGERNON: Lane, you're a perfect pessimist.

LANE: I try my best to give satisfaction, sir.

———

CECILY: I keep a diary in order to enter the wonderful secrets of my life. If I didn't write them down, I should probably forget all about them.

MISS PRISM: Memory, my dear Cecily, is the diary that we all carry about with us.

CECILY: Yes, but it usually chronicles the things that have never happened, and couldn't possibly have happened. I believe that Memory is responsible for nearly all the three-volume novels that Mudie sends us.

MISS PRISM: Do not speak slightingly of the three-volume novel, Cecily. I wrote one myself in earlier days.

CECILY: Did you really, Miss Prism? How wonderfully clever you are! I hope it did not end happily? I don't like novels that end happily. They depress me so much.

MISS PRISM: The good ended happily, and the bad unhappily. That is what Fiction means.

———

ALGERNON: Can't you invent something to get Miss Prism out of the way?

CECILY: Do you mean invent a falsehood?

ALGERNON: Oh! Not a falsehood, of course. Simply something that is not quite true, but should be.

———

ALGERNON: . . . I have something very serious to say to you.

CECILY: Serious?

ALGERNON: Yes, very serious.

CECILY: In that case I think we had better meet in the house. I don't like talking seriously in the open air. It looks so artificial.

———

MISS PRISM: I highly disapprove of Mr. Ernest Worthing. He is a thoroughly bad young man.

CECILY: I fear he must be. It is the only explanation I can find of his strange attractiveness.

MISS PRISM: Cecily, let me entreat of you not to be led away by whatever superficial qualities this unfortunate young man may possess.

CECILY: Ah! Believe me, dear Miss Prism, it is only the superficial qualities that last. Man's deeper nature is soon found out.

MISS PRISM: Child! I do not know where you get such ideas. They are certainly not to be found in any of the improving books that I have procured for you.

CECILY: Are there ever any ideas in improving books? I fear not. I get my ideas . . . in the garden.

MISS PRISM: Then you should certainly not be so much in the open air. The fact is, you have fallen lately, Cecily, into a bad habit of thinking for yourself. You should give it up. It is not quite womanly. . . . Men don't like it.

———

GWENDOLEN: . . . On an occasion of this kind it becomes more than a moral duty to speak one's mind. It becomes a pleasure.

CECILY: Do you suggest, Miss Fairfax, that I entrapped Ernest into an engagement? How dare you? This is no time for wearing the shallow mask of manners. When I see a spade I call it a spade.

GWENDOLEN: I am glad to say that I have never seen a spade. It is obvious that our social spheres have been widely different.

———

ALGERNON: The doctors found out that Bunbury could not live . . . so Bunbury died.

LADY BRACKNELL: He seems to have had great confidence in the opinion of his physicians.

May It Please the Court

SIR EDWARD CARSON: Listen, sir. Here is one of the *Phrases and Philosophies for the Use of the Young* which you contributed: "Wickedness is a myth invented by good people to account for the curious attractiveness of others." You think that true?

WILDE: I rarely think that anything I write is true.

CARSON: "Religions die when they are proved to be true." Is that true?

WILDE: Yes; I hold that. It is a suggestion towards a philosophy of the absorption of religions by science, but it is too big a question to go into now.

CARSON: Do you think that was a safe axiom to put forward for the philosophy of the young?

WILDE: Most stimulating.

CARSON: "If one tells the truth, one is sure, sooner or later, to be found out"?

WILDE: That is a pleasing paradox, but I do not set very high store on it as an axiom.

CARSON: Is it good for the young?

WILDE: Anything is good that stimulates thought in whatever age.

CARSON: Whether moral or immoral?

WILDE: There is no such thing as morality or immorality in thought. There is immoral emotion.

CARSON: "Pleasure is the only thing one should live for"?

WILDE: I think that the realization of oneself is the prime aim of life, and to realize oneself through pleasure is finer than to do so through pain. I am, on that point, entirely on the side of the ancients—the Greeks. It is a pagan idea.

CARSON: "A truth ceases to be true when more than one person believes in it"?

WILDE: Perfectly. That would be my metaphysical definition of truth; something so personal that the same truth could never be appreciated by two minds.

CARSON: "The condition of perfection is idleness: the aim of perfection is youth"?

WILDE: Oh, yes; I think so. Half of it is true. The life of contemplation is the highest life, and so recognized by the philosopher.

CARSON: "There is something tragic about the enormous number of young men there are in England at the present moment who start life with perfect profiles, and end by adopting some useful profession"?

WILDE: I should think that the young have enough sense of humor.

CARSON: You think that is humorous?

WILDE: I think it is an amusing paradox, an amusing play on words.

———

EDWARD CARSON: You are of opinion, I believe, that there is no such thing as an immoral book.

OSCAR WILDE: Yes.

CARSON: May I take it that you think *The Priest and the Acolyte* was not immoral?

WILDE: It was worse; it was badly written.

———

CARSON: This is in your introduction to *Dorian Gray*: "There is no such thing as a moral or an immoral book. Books are well-written or badly written." That expresses your view?

WILDE: My view on art, yes.

CARSON: Then I take it, that no matter how immoral a book may be, if it is well-written, it is, in your opinion, a good book?

WILDE: Yes, if it were well-written so as to produce a sense of beauty, which is the highest sense of which a human being can be capable. If it were badly written, it would produce a sense of disgust.

CARSON: Then a well-written book putting forward perverted moral views may be a good book?

WILDE: No work of art ever puts forward views. Views belong to people who are not artists.

CARSON: A perverted novel might be a good book?

WILDE: I don't know what you mean by a "perverted" novel.

CARSON: Then I will suggest *Dorian Gray* as open to the interpretation of being such a novel?

WILDE: That could only be to brutes and illiterates. The views of Philistines on art are incalculably stupid.

CARSON: An illiterate person reading *Dorian Gray* might consider it such a novel?

WILDE: The views of illiterates on art are unaccountable. I am concerned only with my view of art. I don't care twopence what other people think of it.

CARSON: The majority of persons would come under your definition of Philistines and illiterates?

WILDE: I have found wonderful exceptions.

CARSON: Do you think the the majority of people live up to the position you are giving us?

WILDE: I am afraid they are not cultivated enough.

CARSON: Not cultivated enough to draw the distinction between a good book and a bad book?

WILDE: Certainly not.

CARSON: The affection and love of the artist for *Dorian Gray* might lead an ordinary individual to believe that it might have a certain tendency?

WILDE: I have no knowledge of the views of ordinary individuals.

CARSON: You did not prevent the ordinary individual from buying your books?

WILDE: I have never discouraged him.

———

CARSON: . . . Have you ever adored a young man madly?

WILDE: No; not madly. I prefer love; that is a higher form.

CARSON: Never mind about that. Let us keep down to the level we are at now.

WILDE: I have never given adoration to anybody except myself.

———

WILDE [*responding to Carson's reading of a letter from him to Lord Alfred Douglas*]:. . . I think it is a beautiful letter. It is a poem. I was not writing an ordinary letter. You might as well cross-examine me as to whether *King Lear* or a sonnet of Shakespeare was proper.

CARSON: Apart from art, Mr. Wilde?

WILDE: I cannot answer apart from art.

CARSON: Suppose a man who was not an artist had written this letter, would you say it was a proper letter?

WILDE: A man who was not an artist could not have written that letter.

CARSON: Why?

WILDE: Because nobody but an artist could write it. He certainly could not write the language unless he were a man of letters.

CARSON: I can suggest, for the sake of your reputation, that there is nothing very wonderful in this "red rose-leaf lips of yours."

WILDE: A great deal depends on the way it is read.

CARSON: "Your slim gilt soul walks between passion and poetry." Is that a beautiful phrase?

WILDE: Not as you read it, Mr. Carson. You read it very badly.

————

CARSON [*after reading another Wilde–Douglas missive*]: Is that an ordinary letter?

WILDE: Everything I write is extraordinary. I do not pose as being ordinary, great heavens!. . .

————

CARSON: Was his [Alphonse Conway's] conversation literary?

WILDE: On the contrary, quite simple and easily understood. He had been to school where naturally he had not learned much.

————

CARSON: Do you drink champagne yourself?

WILDE: Yes; iced champagne is a favorite drink of mine—strongly against my doctor's orders.

CARSON: Never mind your doctor's orders, sir!

WILDE: I never do.

———

CHARLES GILL: You made handsome presents to all these young fellows?

WILDE: Pardon me, I differ. I gave two or three of them a cigarette case. Boys of that class smoke a good deal of cigarettes. I have a weakness for presenting my acquaintances with cigarette cases.

GILL: Rather an expensive habit if indulged in indiscriminately, isn't it.

WILDE: Less extravagant than giving jeweled garters to ladies!

———

GILL: What is the "Love that dare not speak its name"?

WILDE: "The love that dare not speak its name" in this century is such a great affection of an elder for a younger man as there was between David and Jonathan, such as Plato made the very basis of his philosophy, and such as you find in the sonnets of Michelangelo and Shakespeare. It is that deep, spiritual affection that is as pure as it is perfect. It dictates and pervades great works of art like those of Shakespeare and Michelangelo, and those two letters of mine, such as they are. It is in this century misunderstood that it may be described as the "Love that dare not speak its name," and on account of it I am placed where I am now. It is beautiful, it is fine, it is the noblest form of affection. There is nothing unnatural about it. It is intellectual, and it repeatedly exists between an elder and a younger man, when the elder man has intellect, and the younger man has all the joy, hope, and glamour of life before him.

That it should be so the world does not understand. The world mocks at it and sometimes puts one in the pillory for it.

———

GILL: I wish to call your attention to the style of your correspondence with Lord Alfred Douglas.

WILDE: I am ready. I am never ashamed of the style of my writings. . . .

GILL: Do you think an ordinarily constituted being would address such expressions to a younger man?

WILDE: I am not, happily, I think, an ordinarily constituted human being.

Bibliography

The following bibliography lists key works consulted in the preparation of this volume.

PRIMARY SOURCES

Edwards, Owen Dudley, ed. *The Fireworks of Oscar Wilde*. London: Barrie & Jenkins, 1989.

Hart-Davis, Rupert, ed. *The Letters of Oscar Wilde*. London: Rupert Hart-Davis, 1962.

Jackson, John Wyse, ed. *The Uncollected Oscar Wilde*. London: Fourth Estate, 1995.

Lucas, E. V., ed. *A Critic in Pall Mall*. London: Methuen, 1919.

Wilde, Oscar. *The Works of Oscar Wilde*. New York: Lamb, 1909.

————. *Oscariana*. London: Arthur L. Humphreys, 1910.

————. *The Complete Works of Oscar Wilde*. New York: Wise, 1927.

————. *The Prose of Oscar Wilde*. New York: Boni, 1935.

————. *The Complete Works of Oscar Wilde*. London: Collins, 1966; New York: HarperPerennial, 1989.

SECONDARY SOURCES

Aldington, Richard. *The Portable Oscar Wilde*. New York: Viking, 1947.

Anderson, Ronald, and Anne Koval. *James McNeill Whistler*. New York: Carroll & Graf, 1994.

Birnbaum, Martin. *Oscar Wilde: Fragments and Memories*. London: Elkin Mathews, 1920.

Brasol, Boris. *Oscar Wilde, the Man, the Artist, the Martyr*. New York: Scribner, 1938.

Douglas, Lord Alfred. *Oscar Wilde and Myself*. New York: Duffield, 1914.

———. *Oscar Wilde: A Summing Up*. London: Gerald Duckworth, 1940; New York: Icon, 1962.

Doyle, Sir Arthur Conan. *Memories and Adventures*. Boston: Little, Brown, 1924.

Ellmann, Richard. *Oscar Wilde*. New York: Knopf, 1988.

Gide, André. *Oscar Wilde: In Memoriam*. New York: Philosophical Library, 1910, 1949.

Harris, Frank. *My Life and Loves*. New York: Grove, 1925, 1953, 1963.

———. *Oscar Wilde*. New York: Dorset, 1930, 1989.

Housman, Laurence. *Echo de Paris*. New York: Appleton, 1924.

Hyde, H. Montgomery. *The Trials of Oscar Wilde*. New York: Dover, 1962, 1973.

———. *Oscar Wilde*. New York: Farrar, Straus and Giroux, 1975.

Ingleby, Leonard Cresswell. *Oscar Wilde*. New York: Appleton, 1908.

Kernahan, Coulson. *In Good Company*. New York: Books for Libraries, 1917, 1968.

Keyes, Ralph. *"Nice Guys Finish Seventh": False Phrases, Spurious Sayings, and Familiar Misquotations*. New York: HarperCollins, 1992.

Le Gallienne, Richard. *The Romantic 90s*. Garden City, New York: Doubleday, 1926.

Leverson, Ada. *Letters to the Sphinx from Oscar Wilde*. London: Duckworth, 1930.

Lewis, Lloyd, and Henry Justin Smith. *Oscar Wilde Discovers America*. New York: Harcourt, Brace, 1936.

Mikhail, E. H. *Oscar Wilde: Interviews and Recollections*. New York: Harper & Row, 1979.

O'Sullivan, Vincent. *Aspects of Wilde*. New York: Holt, 1936.

Pearson, Hesketh, *The Life of Oscar Wilde*. New York: Harper, 1946.

Raymond, Jean Paul (Charles Ricketts). *Oscar Wilde: Recollections*. Bloomsbury: Nonesuch, 1929, 1932.

Redman, Alvin. *The Wit and Humor of Oscar Wilde*. New York: Dover, 1952, 1959.

Rothenstein, William. *Men and Memories*. New York: Coward-McCann, 1931.

Saltus, Edgar. *Oscar Wilde: An Idler's Impression*. Chicago: Brothers of the Book, 1917.

Schmidgall, Gary. *The Stranger Wilde*. New York: Dutton, 1994.

Sherard, Robert Harborough. *Oscar Wilde: The Story of an Unhappy Friendship*. London: Hermes Press, 1902; New York: Haskell, 1970.

————. *The Life of Oscar Wilde*. London: T. Werner Laurie, 1906.

————. *The Real Oscar Wilde*. London: T. Werner Laurie, 1917.

Symons, Arthur. *A Study of Oscar Wilde*. London: Charles J. Sawyer, 1930.

Weintraub, Stanley. *Whistler: A Biography*. London: Weybright & Talley, 1974; New York: Dutton, 1988.

Notes

Only key sources are cited, primary ones whenever possible. Last names and publication date when necessary refer to publications listed in the Bibliography.

The sources will be referred to by the following key word or initial throughout:

SOURCE	KEY
Edwards, *The Fireworks of Oscar Wilde*	Fireworks
Hart-Davis, *The Letters of Oscar WIlde*	L
Jackson, *The Uncollected Oscar Wilde*	U
Wilde, *Oscariana*	Oscariana
Wilde, *The Works of Oscar Wilde*	W
Wilde, *The Prose of Oscar Wilde*	P
Wilde, *The Complete Works of Oscar Wilde* (HarperPerennial)	C

Wilde's major works will be referred to by the following key words:

MAJOR WORK	KEY
The Picture of Dorian Gray	Gray
Vera, or the Nihilists	Vera
The Duchess of Padua	Padua
Salomé	Salomé
Lady Windermere's Fan	Fan
A Woman of No Importance	Woman
An Ideal Husband	Husband
The Importance of Being Earnest	Earnest
Lord Arthur Savile's Crime	Savile
The Canterville Ghost	Ghost
The Model Millionaire	Model
The Remarkable Rocket	Rocket
Impressions of America	Impressions
The Critic as Artist	Critic
The Soul of Man Under Socialism	Soul
The Decay of Lying	Decay
Pen, Pencil and Poison	Pen
The Truth of Masks	Masks
The Portrait of Mr. W. H.	Portrait
A Few Maxims for the Instruction of the Over-Educated	Maxims
Phrases and Philosophies for the Use of the Young	Phrases
The Ballad of Reading Gaol	Gaol
De Profundis	De Profundis

AUTHOR'S NOTE

Shipps: Anthony Shipps. *The Quote Sleuth* (Urbana: University of Illinois Press, 1990), 47.

THE PUZZLE OF OSCAR WILDE

Parker: *The Portable Dorothy Parker* (New York: Viking, 1944), 321; Orwell: George Orwell, *Orwell: The Lost Writings* (New York: Arbor, 1985), 171; by World War II, Pearson 305; Ellmann: Ellmann xvii; Gide: Gide 16; "Somehow or other": to David Hunter Blair, Mikhail 5; Leverson: Leverson 29; Shaw: Redman 30; Beerbohm: Mikhail 273; "Miss Piffle" episode: Pearson 63–4; Shaw had no enemies: Harris (1925) 417, Pearson 140, M 146, George Bernard Shaw, *Sixteen Self Sketches* (New York: Dodd, Mead, 1949), 183; "came to London": Sherard (1906) 105–6, L 173, Gray, C 22; "He would stab": C 665; Kernahan: Kernahan 216–7; "One must have a heart of stone": Leverson 42; Le Gallienne: Le Gallienne 258; Rothenstein: Rothenstein 87–8; "Familiarity": Mikhail 421; "Nothing": Pearson 43; "It is better": Gray, C 147; "I can believe": Gray, C 21; "I throw probability": Doyle 74; "The reason": Gray, C 67; "We think": Gray, C 67; "No man dies": Portrait, C 1201; "Anybody can sympathize": Soul, C 1101–2; fellow passenger: Ellmann 241; "To the world": L 353; "I think": Fireworks 256; "I rarely think": Hyde (1962) 108; Sir Henry Newbolt: Pearson 156; "Men who are dandies": Model, C 220; "kisses and blisses": Padua, C 608; "scribblers and nibblers": U 99; "vice of verbosity": U 83; "If one had the money": Pearson 69; friend's earlier question: Sherard (1906) 179; "Good Americans": Gray, C 43, Woman, C 436, Oliver Wendell Holmes, *The Autocrat of the Breakfast-Table* (Boston: Houghton, Mifflin, 1858, 1889), 125; "Give me the luxuries": Holmes, Ibid. 125, Pearson 43, Redman 67; "I appropriate": Pearson 87; "I wish I'd said that": Ingleby 67, Brasol 147, Weintraub

296, Mikhail 157, Ellmann 133; Whistler on Wilde: Redman 52, Weintraub 303–5, Ellmann 274, 325, Decay, C 972; "Life is never fair": Husband, C 504; "I can resist": Fan, C 388, Keyes 163; Shaw: Keyes 164, *Man and Superman* Act 4; "In this world": Fan, C 417; "sit and chatter": L 255; "Details are always": Gray, C 85; "Details are the only": Savile, C 173; "To be modern": Woman, C 459; "Nothing is so dangerous": Husband, C 514; "The supreme vice": De Profundis, C 874, 896, 916, 953; "Consistency is the last refuge": U 52, Pearson 171; "Not that I agree": Masks, C 1078; Pearson: Pearson 37; "the supreme vice": De Profundis, C 874, 896, 916, 953; "I wrote when": Sherard (1917) 98; "If the poor": Phrases, C 1205; two letters: C 958–69; "The old": Mikhail 248; "Those whom": Maxims, C 1204.

WILDE'S WILDE

French by sympathy: Ellmann 352; *By nature:* L 269; *I am afraid:* Ellmann 39; *I never put off:* Pearson 173; *I am never in:* L 745; *I am one of those:* De Profundis, C 914; *I have blown:* L 237; *I awoke:* De Profundis, C 912–3; *Praise makes me humble:* O'Sullivan 5; *Where will:* Mikhail 469; *The three women:* O'Sullivan 18; *While the first editions:* Pearson 215; *If I were:* Mikhail 18; *I have:* Saltus 20; *Between me and life:* Mikhail 162; *I like to do:* Rocket, C 315; *I like hearing:* Rocket, C 316; *Geniuses . . . are always:* Husband, C 513; *I am always thinking:* Rocket, C 313; *If life be:* De Profundis, C 917; *I filled my life:* De Profundis, C 917; *Whatever my life:* L 648; *My record:* L 515; *God would:* Padua, C 583; *I must say:* De Profundis, C 912; *A patriot:* L 705; *I entered:* Gide 23; *I am not a scrap:* L 581.

THE ANECDOTAL WILDE

Full Name: Kernahan 208; *Suspense:* James Sutherland, ed., *The Oxford Book of Literary Anecdotes* (London: Oxford University Press, 1975), 299;

Like Mother: Sherard (1906) 136, Sherard (1917) 63; *High Standards:*
Mikhail 4, 169, 444, 469, Brasol 44, Pearson 29, Ellmann 45; *Fame:*
Pearson 44, Ellmann 109; *Path to the Stars:* Brasol 165, Lewis 21–2,
Pearson 39; *Altruism:* Hesketh Pearson, *Gilbert, His Life and Strife* (New
York: Harper, 1957), 110; *God Save the Queen:* Redman, 23; *Touché:*
Birnbaum 29; *Hard of Hearing:* Harris (1925) 416, O'Sullivan 59, Pearson
28, Ellmann 85, Fireworks 32; *Literary Worship:* Pearson 165–6; *Hurt
Feelings:* Le Gallienne 263–5; *Good Manners:* Mikhail 285–6; *Economy:*
Pearson 199; Gray, C 52; *Favorite Topic:* Fireworks 15, Anderson 253–4,
Weintraub 243–4, Pearson 86, Ellmann 271; *Elocution:* Sherard (1917)
288; *Customs Declaration:* Lewis 35, Pearson 53; *Disappointment I:* Lewis
32, Mikhail 38, Pearson 53, Ellmann 158; *Disappointment II:* Impressions,
W (Volume Eleven) 254, Lewis 163, Pearson 59, Ellmann 239; *Weather
Forecast:* Pearson 173; *Royal Rebuke:* O'Sullivan 197; *Heavenly:* Ellmann
198; *Underwhelmed:* Lewis 189, 210, Pearson 60; *On Second Thought:* Lewis
254, Pearson 62; *Wilde's West:* Impressions, W (Vol. Eleven) 258, Lewis
310, Fireworks 47; L 110–2, Birnbaum 23–4, Ellmann 204–5; *Postwar
Blues:* Impressions, W (Vol. Eleven) 259–60, Lewis 396, Pearson 67,
Fireworks 48; *Signs of Success:* Frank Harris (1925) 416, Brasol 98,
Mikhail 32, 215, L 86; *Artistic Integrity:* Saltus 14–5; *Location, Location:*
Sherard (1902) 25–6; *Risk:* Rothenstein 93, Pearson 74; Ellmann 350;
Wildly Bourgeois: Rothenstein 88–9, Mikhail 160–1, Pearson 71; *Self-
Esteem:* O'Sullivan 62; *The Taxman Cometh:* Le Gallienne 259, Pearson
106; *Domestic Tragedy:* Saltus 15; *Prayers:* Mikhail 155, Schmidgall 316;
Bedevilment: Mikhail 161, Ellmann 313; *Plagiarism:* Mikhail 245, Pearson
218; *Secret Society:* Mikhail 211–2, Pearson 198; *Recipe for Success:* Pearson
227; *Uncanny Resemblance:* Pearson 228; *Best Books:* Pearson 174; *Sanity:*
Mikhail 384; *Popularity:* Rothenstein 213, Pearson 160; *Yankee Go Home:*
Fairfax Downey, *Richard Harding Davis* (New York: Scribner 1933), 112;
Familiarity Breeds Contempt: Levenson 25, Pearson 174; *Gag Order:* Pearson
176; *Good Value:* Sherard (1917) 40, Pearson 243–5, Ellmann 446; *Hard*

Labor: Sherard (1902) 72, Sherard (1906) 273, Ellmann 221; *Household Name:* Sherard (1902) 192, Sherard (1906) 278, Pearson 276; *Royal Treatment:* Pearson 281, De Profundis, C 937; *Tactlessness:* Mikhail 340, Pearson 295; *Kindness:* Pearson 302–3; *Redemption:* Hyde (1975) 330, Ellmann 539–40; *Last Words:* Sherard (1906) 421, Raymond 59, L 848, *New York Times* 10/14/82, Sherard (1917) 330, Ellmann 581.

OSCARIANA

ACTING

I love: Gray, C 70; *Why should:* U 82; *Anybody can:* Fireworks 195.

AGE

Men become: Fan, C 392; *The old should:* Mikhail 248; *I always contradict:* Gray, C 163; *As soon as:* Fan, C 400; *Those whom . . . die old:* Sherard (1917) 7; *Those whom . . . grow young:* Maxims, C 1204; *Young men want:* Gray, C 37; *The old believe:* Phrases, C 1206; *The tragedy:* Gray, C 162; *The secret:* Gray, C 73–4; *Youth smiles:* Gray, C 125; *It's absurd:* Gray, C 163; *I have never:* L 181; *We never:* Gray, C 32; *To get back one's:* Gray, C 44; *To get back my:* Gray, C 162.

ALTRUISM

The majority: Soul, C 1079; *The desire:* Critic, C 1042; *One can:* Gray, C 84; *Conscience and cowardice:* Gray, C 22; *The mere existence:* Critic, C 1024; *Self-sacrifice:* Husband, C 533; *Good intentions:* Oscariana 48; *Whenever a man:* Gray, C 66; *It takes:* Fan, C 403; *Philanthropy seems:* Husband, C 487; *Philanthropic people:* Gray, C 40; *People are:* Lucas 209; *Charity creates:* Soul, C 1079.

AMERICA

English people: U 36; *We have:* Canterville, C 194; *America has never:*

Fireworks 72, Lewis 282; *It is a vulgar error:* Ellmann 166; *America is one:* Lewis 181; *America is the noisiest:* Impressions, W (Vol. Eleven) 252; *One is impressed:* Impressions, W (Vol. Eleven) 253–4; *Bulk is:* Lewis 153; *Everybody seems:* Impressions, W (Vol. Eleven) 252; *I am told:* Gray, C 40; *The people of America:* Lewis 227; *In America the President:* Soul, C 1094; *In America the young:* U 36; *The American child:* Fireworks 74; *There at any rate:* Impressions, W (Vol. Eleven) 262; *In America there is:* Lewis 281; *In going to America:* Impressions, W (Vol. Eleven) 262; *It is impossible:* Lewis 372–3; *The Americans are the best:* Impressions, W (Vol. Eleven) 262.

AMERICANS

All Americans: Woman, C 453; *The American woman:* Mikhail 104; *Many American ladies:* Canterville, C 194; *American girls:* Impressions, W (Vol. Eleven) 261; *American women:* U 37; *For him:* Fireworks 71, Lewis 152; *The telephone:* Fireworks 70; *Real experience:* Lewis 153; *The American man:* Fireworks 71; *If the Americans:* Impressions, W (Vol. Eleven) 251.

APPAREL

A man is called: Soul, C 1101; *Every right article:* Fireworks 51–2; *All costumes:* Fireworks 54; *Cavaliers and Puritans:* Pearson 166; *The artistic feeling:* Fireworks 88; *One should either:* Phrases, C 1206; *The only way:* Phrases, C 1205; *The imagination:* L 284; *It is really:* Fireworks 80–1; *Tails have no place:* Fireworks 51; *With an evening coat:* Gray, C 21.

APPEARANCES

It is only: Gray, C 32; *Being natural:* Gray, C 20; *Perhaps one never:* Gray, C 134; *Man is least:* Critic, C 1045; *A mask tells:* Pen, C 995; *The truth about:* Mikhail 171; *I think a man:* Ellmann 301.

ART

Art is not: U 183; *Art is the mathematical:* Ellmann 238; *It is through*

Art: Critic, C 1038; *Art is what makes:* U 21; *The secret:* Mikhail 69, U 28; *Life imitates art:* Decay, C 992; *It is the spectator:* Gray, C 17; *The work of art:* Soul, C 1096; *The meaning:* Critic, C 1029; *That is the mission:* Mikhail 99, Lewis 374; *To reveal art:* Gray, C 17; *The aim of art:* Mikhail 247; *There are works:* Gide 12; *There is no mood:* Critic, C 1035; *Art is the one thing:* U 118, Ellmann 181; *All good work:*, U 124; *The public make use:* Soul, C 1092; *The one thing:* Soul, C 1091; *A fresh mode:* Soul, C 1092; *Popularity is the crown:* U 123; *No art is better:* Mikhail 71, Lewis 243; *It is very curious:* L 823; *All bad art:* De Profundis, C 941; *It is always:* Critic, C 1053; *The best that one:* Critic, C 1028; *All art is quite:* Gray, C 17; *All art is immoral:* Critic, C 1039; *Art must be loved:* Mikhail 63; *The sign of a Philistine:* U 126; *No art ever survived:* Mikhail 247; *Whenever a community:* Soul, C 1090; *There are two ways:* Critic, C 1047; *It is only an auctioneer:* Critic, C 1047; *Diversity of opinion:* Gray, C 17; *Art should always:* Raymond 34.

ARTISTS

Artists, like: U 17, Lewis 58; *A really great artist:* Critic, C 1053; *The moment that:* Soul, C 1090; *Alone, without:* Soul, C 1090; *Creation for the joy:* Mikhail 242; *When critics disagree:* Gray, C 17; *The true artist:* Soul, C 1092; *Bad artists:* Critic, C 1054; *A true artist:* Soul, C 1097; *Most of our modern:* Decay, C 989; *The only thing:* Maxims, C 1203; *The more the public:* Mikhail 246; *The English public:* Ellmann 352; *To call an artist:* Soul, C 1093; *How can a man:* Housman 29; *No artist desires:* Gray, C 17; *No artist has ethical:* Gray, C 17; *Insincerity and treachery:* Portrait, C 1171; *Vice and virtue:* Gray, C 17; *The young artist:* U 129; *Nothing . . . is more dangerous:* U 123; *No great artist:* Decay, C 988; *The greatest artists:* O'Sullivan 204; *The only artists:* Gray, C 54–5; *Only mediocrities:* L 372, Fireworks 220; *In New York:* U 42; *For an artist:* U 31.

BEAUTY

The desire for: Mikhail 41; *When the result:* Fireworks 114; *The best service:* Mikhail 68; *Beauty, like Wisdom:* Fireworks 183; *Those who do not:* Decay, C 990; *Devotion to beauty:* U 21; *Beauty is a form:* Gray, C 31; *Beauty has:* Critic, C 1030; *Philosophies fall:* U21; *All beautiful things:* Pen, C 996; *Beauty is the only:* U 21; *No object is:* U 129; *I have found:* Ellmann 262; *Utility will:* U 107; *Good machinery:* U 109; *The reason:* U 27; *Aestheticism is:* Ellman 159; *Aesthetics, like:* Critic, C 1058; *Aesthetics are:* Critic, C 1058; *Even a color-sense:* Critic, C 1058.

CLASS

It is only: Phrases, C 1205; *If the lower:* Earnest, C 322; *Each class preaches:* Pearson 177; *There is only:* Soul, C 1085; *Extravagance is:* Mikhail 215; *Romance is:* Model, C 219; *As for the virtuous:* Soul, C 1081; *We are often told:* Soul, C 1081; *To recommend thrift:* Soul, C 1081; *Why should they:* Soul, C 1081; *The real tragedy:* Gray, C 69; *The poor are wiser:* De Profundis, C 911; *Those who have much:* De Profundis, C 914; *I quite sympathize:* Gray, C 23; *A grande passion:* Gray, C 49–50; *There is always:* Vera, C 676; *Study the Peerage:* Woman, C 461.

COMMON SENSE

The inherited: Gray, C 138; *The growth of:* Decay, C 990; *Common sense is:* Fireworks 218; *Anybody can have:* Rocket, C 313; *I love superstitions:* Fireworks 218; *Nowadays most people:* Gray, C 44.

CONFORMITY

While to: Soul, C 1087; *People . . . go through:* Soul, C 1087; *Most people:* De Profundis, C 926; *Selfishness is not:* Soul, C 1101; *It is not selfish:* Soul, C 1101.

CONVERSATION

Conversation is: Fireworks 76; *Ultimately the bond:* De Profundis, C 880; *Conversation should:* Critic, C 1032; *The state of the weather:* U 85; *The art of conversation:* U 86; *Learned conversation:* Critic, C 1015; *Recreation, not instruction:* U 84; *The maxim:* U 86; *One wants something:* Earnest, C 329; *Nobody, even in the provinces:* U 84; *In the case of:* U 86; *A man who can dominate:* Woman, C 459; *I adore them:* Woman, C 441; *One should never:* Maxims, C 1204; *It is a very dangerous:* Husband, C 490; *It is only the intellectually lost:* Gray, C 25; *I dislike arguments:* Earnest, C 379; *Arguments are extremely vulgar:* Rocket, C 315.

CONVICTION

The man who sees: Critic, C 1047; *One should never:* Woman, C 437; *To believe:* Pearson 166; *I never approve:* Gray, C 66; *The things one feels:* Gray, C 161; *A thing is not:* Portrait, C 1161; *No man dies:* Portrait, C 1201.

CRIME AND PUNISHMENT

Murder is: Gray, C 160; *There is no:* Pen, C 1008; *Starvation:* Soul, C 1088; *A community:* Soul, C 1087–8; *As one reads:* Soul, C 1087–8; *The more punishment:* Soul, C 1088; *The criminal classes:* Maxims, C 1204; *Crime belongs:* Gray, C 160; *To turn:* De Profundis, C 933; *Reformation:* Critic, C 1053; *It is not:* Letter to Editor of *Daily Chronicle,* C 962; *The only really:* Letter to Editor of *Daily Chronicle,* C 961; *Prison-life:* L 514; *To those who are:* De Profundis, C 937; *The most terrible:* De Profundis, C 921.

CRITICISM

Criticism is: Ellmann 51; *There has never:* Critic, C 1021; *The highest:* Critic, C 1027; *The censure:* Lucas 203; *The moment:* Mikhail 239.

CRITICS

The critic: L 269; *The true critic addresses:* U 17; *The true critic is:* U 145; *The first duty:* U 17; *Critics rarely:* Mikhail 188; *It is exactly:* Critic, C 1054; *Technique is really:* Critic, C 1054; *It is only:* Critic, C 1033; *A critic should:* Fireworks 168; *The primary aim:* Ellmann 143; *I am always:* Critic, C 1027–8; *No publisher:* L 262.

CRITIQUES

The best play: Mikhail 285; *It is a thoroughly:* Fireworks 69; *As a general rule:* Fireworks 89; *Astray:* Fireworks 63; *Andiatoroctè:* Lucas 208; *Mr. Whistler . . . has:* Fireworks 73; *Mr. Whistler always:* U 137; *That he is:* U 50; *As for borrowing:* L 254, Weintraub 305; *{George Meredith}:* Decay, C 976; *Meredith is:* Critic, C 1013; *M. Zola:* Decay, C 974; *{Guy de Maupassant}:* Decay, C 974; *Mr. Henry James:* Mikhail 178; *{Rudyard Kipling}:* Critic, C 1055; *Longfellow is:* Mikhail 384; *Longfellow has:* U 92; *In his very rejection:* Fireworks 111.

DANGER

To elope: Woman, C 434; *Every profession:* Mikhail 232; *How fond:* Gray, C 154; *An idea:* Critic, C 1044; *Everything is:* Husband, C 504; *The one advantage:* Woman, C 434.

DEFINITIONS

Scandal: Fan, C 416; *Tact:* Fireworks 84; *Cynicism:* Oscariana 31; *What is:* Fan, C 416; *The sentimentalist:* De Profundis, C 946; *A sentimentalist . . . is a:* Fan, C 418; *A sentimentalist is simply:* De Profundis, C 946; *Experience:* Fan, C 418; *Caricature:* Lewis 55; *Indifference:* Vera, C 664; *Democracy:* Soul, C 1087.

DESCRIPTIONS

He is a typical: Husband, C 518; *A red-cheeked:* Gray, C 135; *He hasn't:* Pearson 171; *He is old enough:* Pearson 171; *Like all people:* Gray, C 42; *A man with a hideous:* Woman, C 449; *Many a woman:* Fan, C 390; *She wore:* Husband, C 508; *She behaves:* Gray, C 40; *She was a curious:* Gray, C 47; *When she is:* Gray, C 136; *She tried:* Gray, C 47; *An over-dressed:* Gray, C 135; *She was usually:* Gray, C 47; *She was one:* Rocket, C 311; *{She} talks more:* Husband, C 518; *A dowdy:* Gray, C 135.

DISSENT

Discontent: Woman, C 456; *Disobedience:* Soul, C 1081; *In art:* U 4; *Agitators are:* Soul, C 1082.

DREAMING AND ACTION

It is: Le Gallienne 253; *A dreamer:* Critic, C 1058; *Society:* Critic, C 1039; *The one person:* Critic, C 1023; *It {action}:* Critic, C 1023; *Action . . . becomes:* Critic, C 1023; *We are never:* Critic, C 1040.

DUTY

Duty is: Woman, C 456; *Duty . . . merely:* Soul, C 1100; *My duty is:* Husband, C 541; *My duty to:* Gide 15; *A sense of duty:* Oscariana 49; *People are afraid:* Gray, C 29; *The first duty:* Phrases, C 1205; *A woman's first duty:* Husband, C 532.

EDUCATION

Nothing that: Critic, C 1016, Maxims, C 1203; *Fortunately:* Earnest, C 332; *Just as:* Critic, C 1043; *Everybody who is:* Decay, C 971; *In examinations:* Phrases, C 1205; *Examinations are:* Gray, C 38; *People never think:* Earnest, C 354; *We teach people:* Oscariana 13; *In the summer:* Fireworks 125; *Give children:* Lewis 247; *Children have:* Impressions, in W (Vol. Eleven) 261; *I would have:* U 189; *A school:* Pearson 106.

EMOTION

Emotion for: Oscariana 61; *The secret:* Woman, C 464; *There is always:* Gray, C 76; *It is only:* Gray, C 89; *I cannot repeat:* Gray, C 90; *One of the facts:* L 143.

ENGLAND

Beer: Gray, C 147; *We are in:* Gray, C 119; *In England:* Husband, C 507; *The English public:* Critic, C 1009; *{The English}:* Raymond 27; *To disagree:* U 8; *The English public, as:* Fireworks 167; *Of all people:* Gray, C 45; *One should not:* Fireworks 62; *There are only:* Pearson 310; *We have been able:* Soul, C 1091; *If the English:* Soul, C 1084; *England never appreciates:* Mikhail 45, Lewis 65; *The English mind:* Critic, C 1057; *We were delighted:* Mikhail 40, Lewis 46.

FACTS

If something: Decay, C 973; *Facts are not:* Decay, C 980; *The ancient histo-rians:* Decay, C 972; *In the works:* Decay, C 980; *In the wild:* Gray, C 25.

FAMILY

A family: Vera, C 675; *Fathers:* Husband, C 538; *Families are:* Husband, C 486.

FASHION

Fashion is merely: Ellmann 261; *Fashion is what:* Husband, C 522; *From the sixteenth:* Fireworks 83; *There are fashions:* Pen, C 997.

FRIENDS AND ENEMIES

An acquaintance: Husband, C 486; *Laughter:* Gray, C 22; *Friendship is:* Maxims, C 1203; *I always like:* Gray, C 40; *It is a very:* Rocket, C 314; *At the holy:* Pearson 317; *One has a right:* Gray, C 118; *Formal courtesies:* De Profundis, C 877; *What is the good:* Fireworks 93; *I choose:* Gray, C 23; *Be careful:* O'Sullivan 82; *Next to having:* Lewis 215; *I would sooner:* Vera, C 665; *Every effect:* Gray, C 149.

GENERATIONS

Children begin: Woman, C 457, 480; *Few parents:* Earnest, C 338; *There are:* Husband, C 517; *There is:* Vera, C 666; *The longer:* Gray, C 50; *It is enough:* Pearson 125; *No age:* Lucas 200.

GEOGRAPHY

The two: U 194; *Chicago:* U 36; *It is:* Gray, C 159; *San Francisco:* Mikhail 82; *California:* Lewis 306; *In no place:* Lewis 263; *When I look:* Lewis 420; *This grey:* Gray, C 49; *London:* Fan, C 422; *While in London:* Mikhail 170; *The great superiority:* O'Sullivan 64; *We Irish:* Mikhail 147; *If one could:* Husband, C 533; *I don't like:* L 787; *A map:* Soul, C 1089.

GOVERNMENT

In an evil: P 339; *All modes:* Soul, C 1087; *Life under:* Mikhail 115; *Now that:* Husband, C 485; *Only people:* Husband, C 539; *There is:* Soul, C 1099; *There are three:* Soul, C 1099; *Those who try:* Critic, C 1043; *One who is:* Soul, C 1099; *It is indeed:* Mikhail 240–1; *I like:* Padua, C 630; *To be entirely:* De Profundis, C 891; *All authority:* Soul, C 1087; *Wherever:* Soul, C 1084.

HISTORY

History is: Fan, C 416; *The details:* Critic, C 1021; *History never:* Ellmann 106; *Anybody can:* Critic, C 1023; *The one duty:* Critic, C 1023; *We cannot:* Pen, C 1008; *To give:* Critic, C 1015.

HUMAN NATURE

The more one: Decay, C 975; *The only thing:* Soul, C 1100; *The systems:* Soul, C 1100; *I will predict:* Ellmann 111; *The real fool:* De Profundis, C

874; *To know anything:* Critic, C 1040; *The great things:* Portrait, C
1161–2; *Find expression:* Critic, C 1052; *Every little action:* De Profundis, C
913; *The only thing:* Fireworks 124; *There is a luxury:* Gray, C 81;
Humanity will: Critic, C 1009; *The reason:* Gray, C 67; *We think:* Gray, C
67; *It is what:* O'Sullivan 53; *Great antipathy:* O'Sullivan 36; *Whenever:* De
Profundis, C 939; *It is in:* Gray, C 29; *Each man:* L 266; *We are each:*
Padua, C 641; *Each of us:* Gray, C 122.

HUMOR

Even in: L 541; *Humanity:* Gray, C 44; *Laughter:* L 767; *Where one
laughs:* L 744; *The world:* Woman, C 462; *You can produce:* L 143.

INTELLECT

To expect: Husband, C 526; *Intellect . . . destroys:* Gray, C 19; *Thinking is:*
Decay, C 971; *All thought:* Woman, C 464; *Thought is:* Critic, C 1016;
While, in: Critic, C 1039; *To do nothing:* Critic, C 1039.

JOURNALISM

Bad manners: Mikhail 249, Lewis 32; *Modern journalists:* Soul, C 1093;
There is much: Critic, C 1048; *Journalists record:* Pearson 222; *The journalist:*
Mikhail 242; *In centuries:* Soul, C 1095; *Spies are:* Husband, C 528; *The
conscience:* Lewis 177; *In the old days:* Soul, C 1094.

LIFE

Life is terribly: Critic, C 1034; *Life is much:* Vera, C 665; *Life is never:*
Husband, C 504; *Life goes faster:* Decay, C 992; *Life itself:* Pen, C 995; *The
aim of life:* Gray, C 29; *To live:* Soul, C 1084; *There are:* Vera, C 663; *One
should live:* Ellman 580; *One can live:* Vera, C 684; *We can have:* Gray, C
149; *Don't tell me:* Gray, C 137; *To become:* Gray, C 91; *Life cheats:* Gide 35;
What a pity: Fan, C 420; *For he who lives:* Gaol, C 853.

LITERATURE

Literature always: Decay, C 983; *There is no:* Ellmann 252; *French prose:* U 63; *Anybody can write:* Critic, C 1022; *Many a young man:* Decay, C 973; *I hate vulgar:* Gray, C 147; *It is hard:* Mikhail 379; *Are there not:* Critic, C 1037; *It was said:* U 163; *A steady course:* U 163; *The only form:* Fireworks 79; *To introduce:* Mikhail 241; *If a novelist:* Decay, C 975; *There is a great deal:* P 539; *To know the vintage:* Critic, C 1022; *If one cannot:* Decay, C 977; *There is no such thing as a moral:* Gray, C 17; *The books that:* Gray, C 163; *The fact of a man:* Pen, C 1007; *The Celtic element:* Fireworks 88; *There is no such thing as Shakespeare's:* Critic, C 1034; *Schopenhauer:* Decay, C 983; *No one survives:* U 92; *There is always:* Fireworks 81.

LOVE

All love: Woman, C 480; *Misunderstanding:* Fireworks 75; *Love is not:* Rocket, C 311; *True love suffers:* Rocket, C 311; *To be in love:* Gray, C 62; *I cannot live:* L 644; *Love does not traffic:* De Profundis, C 899; *Love makes:* Gray, C 63; *Love can:* L 577; *Love is the sacrament:* Padua, C 609; *Love is merely:* Padua, C 609; *Everyone is worthy:* De Profundis, C 930–1; *It is not the perfect:* Husband, C 521; *Love can heal:* L 567; *It is love:* Husband, C 511; *Each time that one loves:* Gray, C 149; *Those who are faithful:* Gray, C 25–6; *Faithfulness:* Gray, C 50; *What a fuss:* Gray, C 37; *Lust:* Portrait, C 1186; *It is difficult:* Critic, C 1013; *Yet each man:* Gaol, C 844; *One should always:* Woman, C 461.

MARRIAGE

The proper basis: Savile, C 172; *Married life:* Gray, C 159; *The real drawback:* Gray, C 66; *How marriage ruins:* Fan, C 416; *The happiness of:* Woman, C 461; *Every experience:* Gray, C 66; *The one charm:* Gray, C 20; *The world has grown:* Fan, C 400; *Marriage is hardly:* Gray, C 65–6; *The American freedom:* Fireworks 72, Lewis 153–4; *Divorces are made:* Earnest, C 323; *It's most dangerous:* Fan, C 400; *Nowadays everybody:* L 584;

Twenty years: Woman, C 440; *Girls never marry:* Earnest, C 323; *Men marry:* Woman, C 460; *When a woman:* Gray, C 136.

MEN AND WOMEN

Men know: Woman, C 478–9; *Women are never:* Husband, C 533; *The soul of woman:* Mikhail 104; *Women love us:* Gray, C 137; *They {women}:* Fan, C 416; *The only way:* Gray, C 83; *Women are not meant:* Husband, C 548; *When a man does:* Earnest, C 369; *Talk to every woman:* Woman, C 460; *When a man has:* Husband, C 533; *A man can:* Gray, C 137; *Men always want:* Woman, C 446; *There is only one:* Husband, C 534; *Men when they woo:* Padua, C 594; *Between men and women:* Fan, C 404; *Wicked women:* Fan, C 415; *The amount:* Earnest, C 327; *Every woman is a rebel:* Woman, C 460; *If you want to know:* Woman, C 460; *Women have a wonderful instinct:* Husband, C 503; *No woman should ever:* Earnest, C 376; *One should never:* Woman, C 442; *It is only:* Padua, C 635; *Crying is the refuge:* Fan, C 392; *The one charm:* Gray, C 85; *Women defend themselves:* Gray, C 59; *If a woman:* Fan, C 410; *There's nothing:* Fan, C 417; *Perplexity:* Oscariana 36; *No man has any:* Woman, C 460.

MISCELLANY

It is always nice: Husband, C 523; *Three addresses:* Earnest, C 373; *The man who possesses:* Lucas 197; *A man whose desire:* De Profundis, C 934; *Each of the professions:* Critic, C 1042; *Even the disciple:* Maxims, C 1204; *Every great man:* Critic, C 1010; *Everyone should keep:* Leverson, 54; *I never travel:* Earnest, C 363; *I only care:* L 739; *One can survive:* Woman, C 442; *We are all:* Fan, C 417; *Between the famous:* De Profundis, C 917; *Knaves nowadays:* Padua, C 622; *Formerly we used:* U 96; *To make a good salad:* Vera, C 663; *Nothing looks:* Savile, C 168; *Fan, C 406; There are many things:* Gray, C 50; *There is always something:* Gray, C 53; *The real tragedies:* Gray, C 84; *Why is it:* L 629.

MISFORTUNE

Misfortunes: Fan, C 394; *One needs:* Ellmann 541; *To live:* Mikhail 355; *The happy people:* Oscariana 6–7; *What seem:* Earnest, C 347; *What fire:* Gray, C 138; *Suffering is a terrible:* L 567; *Suffering and:* Letter to *Daily Chronicle,* C 962; *The secret:* De Profundis, C 920; *While to propose:* De Profundis, C 935; *There is no truth:* De Profundis, C 920; *Sorrow, being:* De Profundis, C 919; *Behind Joy:* De Profundis, C 920.

MODERATION

Moderation: Gray, C 138; *Nothing is good:* Ellmann 268; *All excess:* Fireworks 168; *Nothing succeeds:* Woman, C 464.

MODERNITY

Pure modernity: Decay, C 976; *Modernity of form:* Decay, C 977; *To be modern:* Woman, C 459; *Nothing is:* Husband, C 514; *It is only:* Decay, C 991.

MODERN LIFE

In modern life: Husband, C 494; *We are born:* Critic, C 1015–6; *We live in an age of:* Critic, C 1042; *We live in an age that:* Gray, C 87; *People should not:* Lewis 178; *The value of:* Lewis 247; *The type-writing:* L 513; *They {automobiles}:* L 828; *The train:* U 108; *Of what use:* Lewis 168; *Why does not:* Mikhail 145.

MOODS

Only one thing: L 185; *You people:* Gray, C 93; *There must be:* Critic, C 1040; *Speaker:* Fireworks 125; *To yield:* Oscariana 45.

MORALITY

Morality is: Husband, C 519; *There is no such thing as morality:* Mikhail 420; *There is no such thing as a good:* Gray, C 28; *Neither art:* Pen, C 1008;

Science is out: Critic, C 1048; *Any preoccupation:* Phrases, C 1205; *Modern morality:* Gray, C 69; *A high moral tone:* Earnest, C 326; *Manners are:* Gray, C 112; *The moral is:* Doyle 74; *I never came:* Pearson 265; *In old days:* Husband, C 495; *{Al}though of all poses:* Critic, C 1042.

MUSIC

Music is the art: U 17; *A quality:* The Burden of Itys, C 743; *Music . . . creates:* Critic, C 1011; *If one plays:* Earnest, C 329; *If one hears:* Gray, C 47; *I like Wagner's:* Gray, C 47; *Musical people:* Husband, C 513.

NATURE

The things: Lewis 350; *In nature:* L 597; *We all look:* De Profundis, C 954; *If Nature had been:* Decay, C 970; *Nature, which makes:* Gide 6; *Nature is no great:* Decay, C 986; *Nature is always:* Decay, C 977; *Nature is elbowing:* Pearson 86; *A thing in Nature:* Fireworks 188; *The more we study:* Decay, C 970; *Art is our spirited protest:* Decay, C 970; *One touch of Nature:* Decay, C 977; *Whenever we have returned:* Decay, C 979; *I hate views:* Ellmann 137; *When I look:* Decay, C 970; *Nobody of any real culture:* Decay, C 986; *At twilight:* Decay, C 992.

PEOPLE

Only dull people: Husband, C 493; *There are only:* Gray, C 73; *All charming people:* Portrait, C 1153; *I never take:* Gray, C 66.

PERSONALITY

Personality is: Soul, C 1086; *One must accept:* Mikhail 351; *One regrets the loss:* Gray, C 159; *Nothing is so fatal:* Oscariana 50.

PLAGIARISM

Accusations: Critic, C 1019; *I can hardly imagine:* L 253; *Of course I plagiarize:* Ellmann 376; *Never say:* Kernahan 209; *It is only:* Lucas 195, Ellmann 133; *True originality:* Fireworks 87.

PLAYS

The actable value: Fireworks 195; *Every word:* U 76; *The tears:* Critic, C 1038; *No spectator:* Soul, C 1097; *I don't believe:* Mikhail 248; *I never write:* O'Sullivan 183; *There are two ways:* Ellmann 561–2; *I am not nervous:* Mikhail 240.

PLEASURE

Pleasure is the only: Phrases, C 1205; *Pleasure is Nature's test:* Soul, 1104; *No civilized man:* Gray, C 69; *What consoles one:* Fan, C 425; *I adore:* Gray, C 36; Woman, C 443, *A cigarette:* Gray, C 70; *Better to take:* Masks, C 1074; *I don't regret:* De Profundis, C 922; *Not happiness:* Gide 15.

POETRY

Poetry is for: U 63; *Poetry should be:* Mikhail 208; *Poetry may be:* U 174; *Lying and poetry:* Decay, C 972; *There seems to be:* Lucas 214; *All bad poetry:* Critic, C 1052; *Every century:* Fireworks 95; *There are two ways:* Pearson 229; *Most people:* Gray, C 52; *Books of poetry:* Fireworks 123.

POETS

When man acts: Critic, C 1024; *Poets are always:* Mikhail 145, Lewis 65; *A poet without:* Fireworks 65; *Little poets:* U 166; *A great poet:* Gray, C 55; *{Poets} know:* Gray, C 25; *A poet can survive:* Fireworks 63.

PRINCIPLES

I like persons: Gray, C 23; *I don't like:* Husband, C 546; *It is personalities:* Gray, C 52.

PUBLIC

The public have: Soul, C 1095; *The public is wonderfully:* Critic, C 1009; *The public is largely:* L 677; *Public Opinion . . . is:* Critic, C 1055–6; *Public opinion exists:* Maxims, C 1203; *I am very fond:* Mikhail 240.

QUIPS

He never: L 630; *He knew:* Gray, C 30; *There are:* Pearson 235; *Whenever people:* Fan, C 416; *My own business:* Fan, C 414; *Nowadays we are all:* Fan, C 386; *To partake:* Earnest, C 353; *When I am in trouble:* Earnest, C 368; *Why don't you ask:* Fan, C 399; *I seem to have heard:* Critic, C 1013; *The simplicity of your character:* Earnest, C 338; *I am a little too old:* Husband, C 497; *I don't at all like:* Husband, C 540; *On the staircase:* Savile, C 168; *Varnishing:* Pearson 86; *I remember a clergyman:* Woman, C 452; *She ultimately:* Husband, C 518; *She tried:* Gray 1, C 22.

REASON

I can stand: Gray, C 43; *Science can:* Husband, C 487; *I wonder who:* Gray, C 36; *One is tempted:* Critic, C 1044; *The fatal errors:* De Profundis, C 894; *It is not logic:* U 86.

RELATIVES

Relations are: Earnest, C 335; *Relations never:* Earnest, C 335; *I can't help:* Gray, C 23; *After a good dinner:* Woman, C 450; *I have never:* Earnest, C 363.

ROMANCE

When one: Gray, C 52; *The worst of:* Gray, C 25; *There is no such:* L 185; *It is very romantic:* Earnest, C 323; *The very essence:* Earnest, C 323; *Lovers are happiest:* Padua, C 596; *The romance:* Lewis 308; *Women . . . spoil:* Gray, C 33; *Every romance:* Mikhail 241; *How silly:* Husband, C 526; *Romance is:* Model, C 219.

SCANDAL

The basis: Gray, C 154; *One should:* Gray, C 82; *I love:* Gray, C 117; *Scandals:* Husband, C 495.

SIN

What is termed: Critic, C 1023; *Sin is:* Gray, C 36; *By its curiosity:* Critic, C 1023–4; *Sins of the flesh:* De Profundis, C 899; *The body sins:* Gray, C 29; *There were sins:* Gray, C 125; *The only horrible:* Gray, C 153; *There is no sin:* Critic, C 1057; *Oh, can it be:* Padua, C 604; *They do not sin:* Padua, C 645; *The sick do not:* Woman, C 475; *Nothing makes:* Gray, C 85; *The only difference:* Woman, C 462.

SINCERITY

A little: Critic, C 1048; *We are dominated:* Critic, C 1057; *What people call:* Critic, C 1048.

SOCIETY

The canons: Gray, C 112; *Society, civilized:* Gray, C 112; *Society is:* Woman, C 460; *Never speak:* Earnest, C 374; *To get into:* Woman, C 460; *{London society}:* Husband, C 484; *Other people are:* Husband, C 522.

SOUL

Those who: Phrases, C 1205; *When one comes:* De Profundis, C 926; *The soul itself:* Portrait, C 1194; *To recognize:* De Profundis, C 934; *Behind the perfection:* U 146.

STYLE

One's style: L 282; *The best style:* U 142; *Style largely depends:* Earnest, C 374; *Sentiment:* Woman, C 459; *In the mode:* Schmidgall 75; *In matters:* Earnest, C 371.

SUCCESS

Success is: L 143; *There is something about:* Husband, C 511; *There is something vulgar:* O'Sullivan 204; *Anybody can:* Soul, C 1101–2.

SUICIDE

Suicide is: Sherard (1902) 41; *Sometimes I think:* L 185.

SYMPATHY

Humanitarian: Critic, C 1042; *The real harm:* Critic, C 1043; *While sympathy:* Soul, C 1102; *It is much:* Soul, C 1079; *All sympathy:* Soul, C 1101.

TALK

Language is: Fireworks 76; *Actions are:* Fan, C 420; *There is no mode:* Critic, C 1023; *Lots of people:* Fireworks 93; *It is very much:* Critic, C 1023; *I love talking:* Husband, C 490; *Whenever people:* Earnest, C 329; *It is much cleverer:* Earnest, C 369; *The only possible:* Mikhail 242.

TEMPTATION

I can resist: Fan, C 388; *The only way:* Gray, C 29; *There are terrible:* Husband, C 506; *Life's aim:* Woman, C 464.

THEOLOGY

The history: Mikhail 231; *Ordinary theology:* Pearson 112; *To die for:* Portrait, C 1200; *Martyrdom:* Portrait, C 1201; *Skepticism:* Gray, C 148; *In a Temple:* Woman, C 440; *Imaginative people:* Sherard (1906) 377–8; *When I think:* De Profundis, C 915; *Everything to be true:* De Profundis, C 915; *Religions die:* Phrases, C 1205; *In matters:* Critic, C 1047; *Religion consoles:* Gray, C 85; *When I think:* Mikhail 25; *The terror:* Gray, C 29; *The Catholic Church:* Ellmann 583; *Catholicism is:* Ellmann 583; *When the gods:* Husband, C 506; *Prayer must never:* Pearson 165; *I think half-an-hour's:* L 21; *Missionaries are:* Le Gallienne 251; *When you convert:* Pearson 211; *It is so easy:* Critic, C 1047; *He who would:* Soul, C 1087; *How else but:* Gaol, C 859; *Where there is:* De Profundis, C 906.

TIME

Time is: Phrases, C 1205; *When one pays:* Husband, C 538; *He was always:* Gray, C 46–7; *I am not:* Earnest, C 376; *No one should:* L 770.

TOWN AND COUNTRY

Town life: Pearson 122; *One can only:* Sherard (1906) 97; *When one is:* Earnest, C 322; *Anybody can be:* Gray, C 157; *It is pure:* Gray, C 134; *I don't think:* Husband, C 532.

TRIVIA

The trivial: De Profundis, C 880; *We should treat:* Mikhail 250; *People are never:* Lucas 207–8.

TRUTH AND LIES

Truth is entirely: Decay, C 981; *The truth is rarely:* Earnest, C 326; *The truth is a thing:* Husband, C 510; *To know the truth:* Critic, C 1047; *The way of paradoxes:* Gray, C 43; *If truth has:* Fireworks 94; *A truth ceases:* Phrases, C 1205; *It is a terrible thing:* Earnest, C 383; *If one tells:* Phrases, C 1205; *To lie finely:* Oscariana 52; *The only form:* Decay, C 990; *The aim:* Decay, C 981; *Society sooner:* Decay, C 981; *If a man:* Decay, C 971.

UNDERSTANDING

What one: Mikhail 82; *The praise:* Mikhail 72; *It is only mediocrities:* Lucas 20; *I live in terror:* Critic, C 1016; *He is fond:* Husband, C 488; *Incomprehensibility:* Ellmann 339; *Only the great:* Phrases, C 1206; *Nowadays to be intelligible:* Fan, C 390.

VANITY

It is curious: L 673; *To love oneself:* Phrases, C 1206, Husband, C 522; *Egotism is not:* Critic, C 1010; *To be an Egoist:* L 590; *Humility:* Ellmann

367; *Conceit is the:* Mikhail 248; *Conceit is one:* Oscariana 45; *The only thing:* Rocket, C 313; *It would be unfair:* Rocket, C 316.

VIEWS

Nothing is: Woman, C 445; *Nothing pains:* Leverson 52; *The ugly:* Gray, C 19; *Industry is:* Phrases, C 1206; *Dullness is:* Phrases, C 1205; *Questions are:* Husband, C 487; *The word "natural":* Oscariana 51; *The word "practical":* Fireworks 51; *Civilization is:* Gray, C 157; *Psychology is:* Pearson 37; *For he:* U 145; *One could:* Gray, C 55; *To have:* Critic, C 1018; *I don't believe:* Ellmann 227; *I have:* Gray, C 67; *It is always:* Portrait, C 1153; *I always:* Husband, C 498; *Never buy:* Pearson 171; *Whenever one:* Earnest, C 362; *People who count:* L 749; *Create yourself:* O'Sullivan 205; *One should absorb:* Gray, C 85; *Details are:* Savile, C 173; *It is only about:* Critic, C 1047; *It is only in:* Soul, C 1082; *One can always:* Schmidgall 123; *It is a very unimaginative:* De Profundis, C 937; *The only things worth:* Oscariana 52; *Nothing is worth:* U 127; *Man can believe:* Pearson 125; *One should always be:* Phrases, C 1205; *Secrecy seems:* Oscariana 45; *Most men and women:* Savile, C 174; *An eternal smile:* Oscariana 11; *Ambition is:* Phrases, C 1205; *Consistency is:* U 52; *We are never:* Critic, C 1045; *It is often said:* Soul, C 1094; *One should always play:* Husband, C 496; *Good resolutions:* Gray, C 84; *There is only:* Gray, C 19; *In this world:* Fan, C 417; *The wellbred:* Phrases, C 1205; *There is no:* Gray, C 153; *Everyone is born:* Woman, C 458; *If a man:* L 169.

VIRTUE

I would sooner: L 686; *Don't be led:* Pearson 170; *You can't:* Woman, C 437; *If you want:* Gray, C 67; *It is a sign:* Mikhail 233; *It is absurd:* Fan, C 388; *What are called:* Fan, C 421; *If one intends:* Oscariana 51; *Nowadays so many:* Fan, C 386; *If you pretend:* Fan, C 387; *Leading a double:* Earnest, C 343; *To be good, according:* Critic, C 1057–8; *To be good is:* Gray, C 69; *One is not:* Mikhail 197; *The best way:* Fireworks 83; *Wickedness is:* Phrases, C

1205; *Good people:* Fan, C 388; *One is punished:* De Profundis, C 916; *If we lived:* Critic, C 1023; *It is a very:* Gray, C 112.

Vulgarity

Vulgarity is: Husband, C 522; *All crime:* Gray, C 160; *As long as:* Critic, C 1057; *It is very vulgar:* Earnest, C 325.

Wealth

What this: Husband, C 504; *Young people:* Ingleby 318, Pearson 153; *Private property:* Soul, C 1083; *The true perfection:* Soul, C 1083; *When one has learnt:* L 575–6; *God used poverty:* L 821.

Work

Work is: Pearson 170; *Man is:* Soul, C 1089; *Hard work:* Rocket, C 317; *Cultivated idleness:* L 269.

Writing

Idleness: Mikhail 242; *Romantic surroundings:* L 520; *The difficulty:* Lucas 210; *Writing to newspapers:* L 279; *Even prophets:* U 144; *To learn:* L 233; *I write because:* L 266; *I don't write:* Mikhail 240, U xviii; *I wrote when:* Mikhail 450.

BYPLAY

Vera, or the nihilists
C 677, C 662.

The Duchess of Padua
C 592, C 629.

Lady Windermere's Fan

C 386, C 389, C 403, C 415, C 415, C 417.

A Woman of No Importance

C 433, C 434, C 435–6, C 436, C 437, C 438, C 440, C 441, C 442, C 445, C 446, C 447, C 449, C 471, C 478–9.

An Ideal Husband

C 486–7, C 489, C 523, C 531, C 516, C 490.

The Importance of Being Earnest

C 327, C 327–8, C 328, C 332, C 333, C 335, C 338–9, C 341, C 354, C 355, C 356, C 364, C 372.

MAY IT PLEASE THE COURT

Hyde (1962) 106, 108–10, 112, 115–7, 121–2, 129, 201–2, 204; Fireworks 255–61; Redman 225–31, 234–5, 237–8, 240–2; Pearson 179–80.

Index